MEEK AMERICANS

& Other European Trifles

By

JOSEPH WARREN BEACH

THE UNIVERSITY OF CHICAGO PRESS
CHICAGO

Composed and Printed By
The University of Chicago Press
Chicago, Illinois, U.S.A.

MEEK AMERICANS

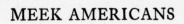

THE UNIVERSITY OF CHICAGO PRESS
CHICAGO, ILLINOIS

—

THE BAKER & TAYLOR COMPANY
NEW YORK

THE CAMBRIDGE UNIVERSITY PRESS
LONDON

THE MARUZEN-KABUSHIKI-KAISHA
TOKYO, OSAKA, KYOTO, FUKUOKA, SENDAI

THE MISSION BOOK COMPANY
SHANGHAI

There is another offence unto Charity, which no Author hath ever written of, and few take notice of; and that's the reproach, not of whole professions, mysteries, and conditions, but of whole Nations, wherein by opprobrious Epithets we miscall each other, and by an uncharitable Logick, from a disposition in a few, conclude a habit in all.

> *Le mutin Anglois, et le bravache Ecossois,*
>   *Et le fol François,*
> *Le poultron Romain, le larron de Gascongne,*
> *L'Espagnol superbe, et l'Aleman yvrongne.*

St. Paul, that calls the Cretians "lyars," doth it but indirectly, and upon quotation of their own Poet. It is as bloody a thought in one way, as Nero's was in another; for by a word we wound a thousand, and at one blow assassine the honour of a Nation.

SIR THOMAS BROWNE, *Religio Medici*

But from that same provision of understanding there springs in us compassion, charity, indignation, the sense of solidarity; and in minds of any largeness an inclination to that indulgence which is next to affection.

JOSEPH CONRAD, *Chance*

VERYBODY knows that we started as an English colony, that our laws are English, that our fare is English meat and potatoes, that a well-dressed American is a man who follows London styles, and that a handsome American is one with features that came over in the Mayflower.

In France I think how much we are like the shrewd and witty Gauls, with their sensitive mouths, their brisk, business-like ways, their disposition to judge a man by his brains. In Italy I feel that we are an Italian people, lean and energetic, good at a bargain, fond of a good time, childlike, and making much of children. In German countries I realize that America is German. So this is German efficiency—this beautiful plumbing, electric lights that work, and thermometers neatly fixed outside each hotel window! And I realize, moreover, that American kindliness is German *Gemütlichkeit.*

A Norwegian governess in a French chateau is a pretty coed in a Minnesota college. She has no secrets from me. A young Swedish count is the best company at Chambord and Cheverny; he speaks the language of London, and his modesty and mannerliness are those of an American college boy. The missionary would have me think that the Chinese people are degenerate and have no virtues—they are dishonest, cruel, licentious, and utterly selfish. But Witter Bynner tells a different story; and he has lived with them, and taken a brother from among them. As for me, "I feel not in myself those common Antipathies that I can discover in others: those National repugnances do not touch me, nor do I behold with prejudice the French, Italian, Spaniard, or Dutch; but where I find their actions in balance with my Countrymen's, I honour, love, and embrace them in the same degree. . . . . I am no Plant that will not prosper out of a Garden. All places, all airs, make unto me one Countrey; I am in Minnesota everywhere, and under any Meridian."[1]

One is saddened by those animosities that flourish about the barriers of tariff and of lan-

[1] Apologies to Sir Thomas Browne.

guage. And yet I know not how to dispense with languages. They are the souls of peoples, and make me love them before ever I have seen Paris or Vienna. Esperanto I cannot stomach; it is a flower without fragrance, an apple without taste. English I love because it is my pipe, and I know how to play upon it. Foreign tongues I love for their very strangeness, and there is none that is not beautiful. Italian is harsh and haughty, with the crack of a pistol shot, and the ceremonial fulness of its Latin inflections. The streets are full of the crackle of mercenary reckonings—*quaranta centesimi, cinquanta centesimi!* It has the pungency of fruits acid and sweet. I have heard in Byzantine Sammarco an old priest in golden vestments speaking to a company of beggars and sobbing madonnas of the *amarezza dolce* of Christ's words. In Santa Maria del Fiore I have heard a crude young priest reciting the triumphs of the Roman church, and I felt that Newman beside him was weak and pale. German is the language for Gurnemanz, and for Schubert's serenading lover. There is no moonlight like Schubert's *Mondenlicht,* no spirit of the woods like Tieck's *Waldeinsamkeit.* French is the tongue for Lamartine and Baudelaire, for songs interpreted by Loeffler and De Bussy:

Il est amer et doux, pendant les nuits d'hiver . . . . .

It is before all the language of the stage, of swift elusive wit and cadenced declamation. It is veiled and resonant, nervous and *nuancé*, and changing as lights upon a fountain. The right Parisian is the choicest music of the modern world, with its vowels melted down and subtly mingled with throaty *r*'s and reedy nasals. It is the voice of thought and of sensation; of flesh caressing spirit, and spirit caressing flesh.

We are the slaves of generalization. A generalization is the truth of this moment, and the falsehood of the next.

Der Mensch ist ungleich, ungleich sind die Stunden.

But how shall we do without generalizing, if only to fix the truth of the moment? These essays are the records of moods, and sometimes contradict each other. So much the better. The only thing I hate is prejudice. The Norman coal-heaver took me for a German: he pressed his cup of cider on me, and hailed me "Kamerad!" I would rather cut my throat than be a cause of more fighting.

January 10, 1925

TABLE OF CONTENTS

MEEK AMERICANS

I

MEEK AMERICANS

ONE is at a loss to know what it is the French love so much in the Americans. It is clearly not our national culture, of which they are so largely unaware. It is not our way of looking at things, at which they can only wonder and smilingly shake their heads. It is not our sentiment, our humor, our political ideas. And yet, with all these abatements, they go on loving us, and one comes to realize in the end that we have one great virtue, and it is for that they love us, as all the world loves us. And our one great virtue is—the dollar.

People talk of the industries and products of France—of wine, and silk, and porcelain, and the modes. The most flourishing of all French industries is the importation of foreigners. And their largest exportation is French culture. It is not the wash of tourists through the grand boulevards and the Rue Scribe that is the most impressive. It is not even the almost complete taking over of the Latin quarter by foreign art students. What is still more striking is the penetration of foreigners into French family life, and that not merely in the neighborhood of the Etoile or the Rue Vavin. What respectable widow of Versailles or Meudon has not her British pensionnaires? What titled family of the Loire does not fill its château with young gentlemen from Colombia, with young ladies from Sweden? What sweet old Norman farm but receives week-end visits from American women running down from Paris? Above all, Americans. For every Britisher, for every Oriental, for every Brazilian, there are two Americans.

And they are people who stay for six months, for a year, for two years. They learn to communicate ideas in the French language, with more or less precision, and, with more or less vagueness, they take in a stock of French ideas to communicate. They return to Kansas or Connecticut shedding light, and they invariably send back twice their own number in search of the same illumination.

Of Americans in Europe there are two main

types: the loud and the meek. The loud is the type most in evidence and that by which we are best known. It is they who make the world think of Americans along with green apples, tin horns, and the rasp of a sawmill. But much more important in the French economy are the meek Americans, of which sect we profess ourselves to be humble members. It is not that we are really so meek. But we are open-minded and curious. We have a kind of anthropological interest in the ways of other peoples. We like to know how they think and feel, and what arrangements they have made for running the social machine. We are even ready to entertain the hypothesis that their ways are in some respects as good as our ways, or at any rate that for themselves they may be supposed to know best what suits them. We are fond of history, and we have had so little of it ourselves that we turn with interest to foreign countries, who have had, perhaps, too much. We stand at gaze before the figure of Saint Louis, and Louis le Grand, and Bonaparte.

Altogether, we are bound to fall under what we may call the "Spell of France." The French have long been busy weaving this spell. They were at one time the greatest nation in Europe, and they even conceived of making themselves the Roman masters of the world. This ambition they could not realize, and they have been gradually losing ground since the days of Louis XIV. But they have never failed to maintain in full vigor, and propagate abroad, the great tradition of Gallic prestige.

Their chief strength lies in their unconsciousness of any culture but their own. In perfect innocence, as it seems, they have declared a boycott on all foreign ideas and inventions. They have made their world, and they go on living in it as complacently as if no other existed. They seem to say that a lady could not walk on any but Louis XIV heels, or sit on any but Louis XV chairs; that a gentleman could not survive any but Gauloise cigarets; that the salvation of Europe is in the secret councils of the Quai d'Orsay; and that society is everywhere built on four main pillars, to wit: the *jeune fille*, the *cocotte*, family affection, and the French triangle.

The French never boast of the superiority of their ways. They simply never bring them into comparison with other people's. Above all, it

never occurs to the French that social life is prac-
ticed in Greenville, Tennessee, and in New Canaan, Connecticut, as infallibly as in Paris or
Limoges. They do not suspect what we know so
well, that the American woman of breeding has
by heart a code as fixed and venerable as that of
the French. She knows how to lay her fork on
her plate, how to receive the young men come to
play tennis with her daughter, and who in a
given situation is the first to leave her card. It is
in Paris and Limoges that Americans of breeding are at fault, and that is because we are so
much concerned not to tread on the toes of our
hosts.

They get the notion that we have no manners, or only bad ones. And we are at little pains
to enlighten them on our own merits. We are
grateful for being taken so graciously into the
family. We do not want to dispute with our
hosts. Especially we are engaged by our national
delicacy of feeling not to be rough with people
who are in a manner dependent upon us. And
then we suffer under the handicap of the foreign
language. We are so liable, in taking issue on
any point, to express ourselves without finesse,

and with a crudeness of emphasis which is not in our intention. So that in general we let them have their own way. We come to them to learn French, and they think we have come to learn the art of living.

And first they address themselves to our supposed Puritanism. They love to sing those snatches of song from their musical shows which will cultivate our sense of humor and lighten up our heavy spirits with equivoque and innuendo. There is nothing of which the French woman is prouder than her freedom from prudery. I asked my hostess whether the French men had the English custom of staying at table after dinner for their cigars and wine. "The men file off to the smoking-room," she said, "and tell dirty stories." And she said it with the satisfaction with which one confesses to his own virtues. This same lady is determined never to let her daughter out of her sight until she is married. But she is content that her daughter shall be present at talk so gross that the American college man is ashamed of listening to it. We tell ourselves that these are more or less matters of convention, and silently continue to prefer our own system. But our French hosts feel that they have given us a touch of social polish.

And then they enlarge on the horrors of American society. A large part of the talk of one hostess was devoted to the subject of divorce, and it would appear that her acquaintance with Americans was almost wholly limited to divorcées, alcoholics, and dope fiends. They were all, it seemed, persons of unusual charm, well provided with dollars, and with the best social connections in New York and Boston, and they had enjoyed her hospitality, and made, indeed, a part of her social circle in Paris. She was evidently proud to know them, but she did deplore the social state of which they were symptomatic. We, who did not know them, were inclined to ask ourselves whether they should really be taken for representative Americans. Our hostess was particularly wordy on the subject of American women: so spoiled, so idle, so irresponsible, so little devoted to their husbands. It was clear from what she said that the women among her American boarders—all of them quite charming and so well connected!—were at the same time strikingly inferior to the French in those virtues which ought to signalize a woman.

And as for our children! It was notorious that Americans went on the principle of letting their children run wild; that obedience, deference, and good manners were things with which we did not concern ourselves in the training of the young. It was unfortunate that her own little girl should have been with us to suggest that children in all countries may be headstrong, petulant, and forward. In this case the little girl was but following her mother's lead in directing us to eat our pie with our fingers instead of with our forks, and what to do between courses with our dirty knives. She had taken in the idea that we were there to be instructed.

In our American code it is not good form to run down the nationality of our guests and friends. And we felt that our hostess might have shown less alacrity in generalizing her views of American manners, especially while we were there.

Certainly the French love us well. They tell us so in so many words. And they imply it in the lavish flattery which they address to us person-

ally. And it is strange that they should resent
so much the comparison of anything French to
anything American. Twice it occurred, during
our stay with a certain family, that some Frenchman was spoken of as reminding one of the best
type of American. The suggestion was scornfully received, and the young American who
made it was given to understand that the two
types were not in any way susceptible of comparison. And yet he had evidently meant it for
a compliment to the Frenchman.

They ought not to find so strange the use of
the word "American" as a general term of commendation, in view of their own similar use of the
word "Parisian." A woman, or a dress, or a work
of art takes rank according as this word is, or is
not, applicable. I remember an occasion when a
Frenchwoman made her comments on the models for dresses appearing in the Sunday supple-
ment of a Kansas City newspaper. The eagerness with which she seized this sheet of pictured
confections suggested that she did not altogether scorn sartorial suggestions emanating
from Missouri. But her first sweeping and somewhat scornful remark was, "Not at all Parisian!"

The dresses were not such as to please her exacting taste. And then she discovered one that was indeed attractive, and she granted, "That is Parisian." And then another, and then another. Out of some dozen models from Kansas City she discovered as many as seven that had the true Parisian style. And I wondered how many she would have found in a similar sheet of Paris models!

Another word of equal breadth is the word *chic*, which has an even greater mystical virtue, and which is particularly handy for knocking down people who do not possess the quality implied. I have generally heard it applied to American women, the intimate friends of the French-woman who used the word. "Oh, yes, Julia is a dear, and I love her sincerely. She is so conscientious, and she has such a good heart! A perfect lady, too—you know the Pitneys are one of the best families of Philadelphia. Pitney, Pitney, and Pitney! I count her one of my best friends. She spends a lot of money on her clothes. To be sure, she has no *chic!*" And suddenly you have the picture of a woman in a hammock, flushed and uneasy in blue satin and expensive lace, who devotes an Oklahoma fortune to making herself a fright. Whereas Julia is a woman remarkable, so far as I could judge, for quiet elegance and style in dress. And you wonder what can be the precise meaning of this mysterious and killing word. You look in vain to your French hostess for an example of *chic*. And you come to the conclusion that the word *chic* is simply the poisoned arrow of her envy.

God save us from generalization! I am sure the woman referred to is not typical of French hostesses in the want of tact with which she betrayed her sense of the superiority of all things French and the inferiority of all things American. But I fear she is typical of a common state of mind, and of a system of cultural browbeating by which many Frenchmen undertake to maintain their moral supremacy over the minds of meek Americans. It is a kind of Poincarism of private life by which, however often their bluff may be called in the world of politics, they continue to demand of their neighbors a slavish reverence for French culture.

French culture is certainly something to be admired, and cultivated people have always been ready and eager to admire it and to love it. In literature, in social custom, in the life of towns, they love it, as they love it in some old Norman church or some fine country-house of Touraine, for its age, its sureness, its refinement, and its sociable humaneness, its eminent suitability to the needs of people living together. It is one of the supreme achievements of European civilization. But after all it is only one among the several great Western cultures: Italian culture, German culture, British culture, American culture. And this is a circumstance of which the French seem unaware. They graciously welcome strangers, generous to share the light which they so largely enjoy. But of the give-and-take of international intercourse they have frequently so little idea. And at last we tire of the one-sidedness of the bargain. We are willing to go a long way to meet them, to make the largest concessions to a people and a social order so much more venerable and distinguished than our own. But we will not—some of us will not—make all the concessions.

You will sometimes encounter an American who has made all the concessions. He is likely to be some kind of an artist, and often a man of talent. He is, let us say, a poet, and he cannot find in Harrisburg the milieu which he needs for developing his genius. He feels that he cannot do his best amid so much ugliness, cannot burn the pure flame of the spirit in an atmosphere so heavy with the fumes of vulgarity and commercialism. He comes to France. He finds there the atmosphere of aesthetic appreciation and endeavor; he finds beauty and an easy, ardent life. He falls in love with French culture; he takes a French mistress; he adopts French ways, and joyously embraces French opinions on every conceivable subject. In everything he agrees with his French mistress. He has the pleasure of hearing her descant daily on the crassness of American ideas and the vulgarity of American manners. And he always says that she is right.

That is, of course, an extreme case of the meekness of Americans. Not many of us yield so completely to our national disposition to self-effacement. But, when it is a question of French culture, some of us are inclined to carry it rather far. Surely we don't want to maintain our love for France at the cost of our own self-respect?

ON THE DEPRAVITY OF
EUROPEANS

II

ON THE DEPRAVITY OF
EUROPEANS

HEY come abroad to study art, but their real passion is for morals. And they never miss an occasion to comment on the moral depravity of European life. What first arouses the indignation of these American women is the art which they come over to study. They go into the public gardens, and they find not merely trees and flowers and fountains—which is quite as it should be —but they find also human figures in marble and bronze, which at once appear to them in the light of persons no better than they should be. Now I hope I recognize the charm of trees and flowers and fountains, all cool and innocent and soothing as a cloister. And I would not look for statues in the north woods. But a garden is another matter; it is humanity's improvement upon nature. Hence the spouting water and the clipped hedges, the bowers and the lovers' walks. And a garden without its statue is like a sentence without its verb. It is like a life without love. And a statue of what? Of Bryan?

In America too, come to think of it, we have statues in our public gardens. But we do not notice them. We do not notice them because they are not good-looking. And they are not good-looking, for one reason, because they are so likely to represent ugly old men in Prince Albert coats. Whereas in European gardens, the heritage of wicked Medicis and Bourbons, they are so much more likely to be Hermes or Aphrodite—in marble!

Ay, there's the rub! They are beautiful, and they are naked. For men and women to go about the streets in such a state would be an offense to decency and even perhaps an incitement to vice. And these critics of morals feel, somehow, that the same rule applies to the gods.

But, my dear Madam, is not the case just the contrary? The gods go naked because we must not do so. We are frail creatures, subject to the law, and accountable to the gods. But the gods are strong and above the law. We live in a world of right and wrong; but they are beyond good and evil. The gods may go anywhere without clothes—oh, for so many reasons! Because they are so good-looking. Because they are not afraid of taking cold. Because they have no reputation to lose. Because we have so great a need of beauty! It is because we are good that we need statues. So many of us have no other occasion to gratify our love of beauty in the human figure! You especially, dear Madam, who are so pure in deed and thought, devoted, it may be, to life-long singleness, or life-long faithfulness to a husband who is so far from being a god. You love roses and lilies and never tire of having them in sight. Would you go through life and never rest your eyes on flowers the most dazzling and seductive yet produced by the gardener Nature?

The queer thing is that, feeling as they do about the use of the human figure in art, my American friends have so little sympathy for the cubists, who have suppressed the human figure altogether or dismembered it quite beyond recognition. There was the director of an art school back home whom I wished to introduce to the art of the moment in Paris. I had been struck with what is called the abstract character of cubist painting; its purity, its sacrifice of the outward sensual aspect in favor of the inward and eternal character of things. And so it was with hopefulness and a great deal of complacency that I took my friend from Marion to the galleries of the New Evangel to view the canvases of Bracque and Léger, of Juan Gris, and Picasso. Here one might revel in patterns as innocuous as a kaleidoscope, wedges and scrolls and cylinders, capricious prisms and cascades of color—the mystic marriage of straight lines and curved—with only here and there a hand or an eye, a stovepipe or a table leg, a melon or a mandolin, to suggest the world of original sin from which the artist had taken his departure.

But instead of being charmed by this chaste reconstruction of the sensible world, my friend was shocked and disgusted as by some exhibition of obscenity. Where I could trace but line and color, she seemed to scent corruption. You could see her wince before the straight lines and veil her eyes before the curved. The uncompromising black surfaces were like so many naked men. She is a woman of liberal views, and she did not use the word, but she seemed to feel obscurely that there was something impious in such an attempt to make over God's world, taking it to pieces and putting it together again according to the whim of the artist. Her Scotch ancestors would have called it sorcery, the squares and circles of necromancy, and they would have burned canvas and painter whose boldness promised an outbreak of the witches' Sabbath. But she is a modern woman, and she contented herself with calling it morbid. She knows what is due to nature. She said she thought it was the work of morons.

It seemed a pity that the director of an art school should dismiss with so little effort at understanding a group of artists who have so long received the serious consideration of competent critics. I thought she might be affected by the vogue which they enjoy among people "in the know." There could hardly be greater evidence of this than the use of their costumes and settings in so many of the representations of the Russian ballet of Monte Carlo. And so I persuaded her to accompany me to a performance in which figured the designs of several of these men, along with the music of their contemporaries and kindred spirits, Milhaud, Satie, Strawinsky. And I think she was a little more favorably impressed with the work of the painters. But this time it was the music that caused her particular distress. There was something about the way these harsh and lively themes dodged in and out and jostled each other that made her nervous. It was no use talking to her of counterpoint and polyphony when her instinct spoke louder of illicit cravings and incestuous unions. More than once she scented syncopation, and she took it for a personal insult. She came away from the Russian ballet more than ever persuaded that European art is degenerate, and she took the next boat home, only stopping long enough to make a sketch of fishing smacks at Paimpol.

It was all very unfortunate. This woman is, I am sure, not insensible to the prestige of success; and here was a school of art about which it was important that she should have some knowledge, as a leader in the movement at home. Things might have gone better if it had not been for an incident of the afternoon. We were strolling in the Luxembourg gardens, admiring the roses and the play of the fountain, when, turn-

ing down an alley, we came upon a couple of
young people seated on a bench. They had their
arms around each other and their faces were
close together. It was very stupid of me, but I
didn't realize how this sight would affect my
companion, and, instead of turning down another path, I kept right on, and—well, she received the blow full in the face. She took one
brief, but intense and comprehensive look, and
then she put up her chin and marched straight
forward with her eyes glued to the statue of
Paul Verlaine.

And I only made things worse by my remarks.
I tried to take the matter lightly, though God
knows I was serious enough.

"People like you and me," said I, "must feel
like intruders in these gardens. They are meant
for children and poets and lovers. It is they who
understand the proper uses of a garden, and they
are the only ones who have any business here.
But still, they never seem to mind us, and it is
such a pleasure to watch them! You know, my
dear Alice" (for we were childhood friends and
always called each other by our given names),
"I sometimes think, my dear Alice, that it is they

who furnish a justification of life, and, as you might say, offer an excuse for all of us. They are like the ten good men who saved the city in the Holy Land; you know, that city that was so wicked. It is what you might call a kind of vicarious salvation. It does one good to come into the gardens at the end of the day and find these things going on. How many a wasted day of one's own is redeemed by other people's kisses! Lovers and poets and children! They really do not mind us in the least. We may look upon them as our monitors, our teachers in the art of living!"

But somehow the more I talked the colder grew the atmosphere between us. "Disgusting!" muttered Alice. "To have one's afternoon spoiled by such an exhibition! So shameless!"

I tried to understand, to meet her halfway. "It is true these are not ladies. Ladies have all sorts of arrangements for meeting in private—taxis and teashops, and the houses of their friends—all sorts of places. But what would you have, in a democracy! These people are no doubt servants, and students, and workingpeople, all that sort of thing. Poor dears! I don't suppose

they have any other place to go. But you know,
my dear Alice, I sometimes think the gardens
are more suited to this sort of thing than any
other place. So retired and sympathetic, with
the children playing so merrily, the poets so
friendly, the sky and lawns so suave and benign,
the statues gleaming from their bosky retire-
ments, the roses and larkspurs so busy with the
same sort of thing. . . . . ''

It was as far as I could get. "Oh, drop it!"
snapped Alice. And ten minutes later she explained: "It's a pity a decent woman can't walk
in the park without having such things thrust in
her face!"

My friends have always a great deal to say
about the "Latin man" and his lack of principle.
They are all agreed that the Latin man is hope-
lessly depraved. And I feel they must be right,
they have taken such pains to find out about him.
Whenever you meet an American woman abroad
you have to spend the night in the music halls
and the dance halls so that she may verify her
theory of Latin morals.

There was the night I spent with Cousin
Rachel in Monte Carlo. Cousin Rachel is the

very nicest of all my relations, and a woman *sans peur et sans reproche*. She has been a good wife to Edward Senior; Edward Junior she has brought up with assiduous devotion and launched him safely on his academic career at Williams. She is a very pretty and a very well-preserved woman, who might well pass for under forty. I think she has a dim sort of idea that she has missed something, and has spent the past year in the capitals of Europe more or less looking for what she has missed. That time in Monte Carlo she was feeling very expansive because she had made a big haul at the Casino, and had the sense—entirely characteristic of her—to come away with the sum intact; and she had insisted that I go with her to the gala dinner at the Café de Paris, along with some friends who had come down from La Turbie. We had a very merry dinner. The tables were gay with flowers and butterflies and parasols and balloons. There were two orchestras, one Russian and one American, but equally jazzy; and the diners took turns with the professionals on the intimate little dancing-platform. Champagne was de rigueur, and everyone began at an early stage to show the heartening effects of the beverage. Of course, I don't mean that anyone in our party showed any undue exhilaration. We were just gay enough to be witty at our own expense, and to feel a genial friendliness toward our neighbors of the evening. I made my literary contribution: "A touch of champagne makes the whole world kin." "Kin-dle!" cried Cousin Rachel gaily, with the prettiest touch of color in her cheeks.

It was well along toward midnight that things began to speed up. The renewed champagne bottles were all that remained of dinner. But now people had put on their colored paper hats and had begun to toot their horns and whistles, and to blow up those funny sausage-shaped balloons, and to pelt one another with those colored paper balls, like so many playful children. It was quite infectious; you simply couldn't resist the temptation to aim at the bald head of that red-faced man in spectacles or into the neck of that broad-shouldered lady with the red coral ornaments in her hair. And even Cousin Rachel was not immune. She picked a man of about her own age, a pleasant-looking man in eyeglasses, who seemed to take much satisfaction in himself. And when he became aware that he was the object of her attentions he smiled with such heightened satisfaction, and with such a cunning, faunlike smile—for Cousin Rachel is always thought a pretty woman—that she could not resist throwing some more. And then he began to return the compliment, and finally left his table to get a better view, and in the end he came up and asked for a dance. And he was so polite, and so deferential toward me as her male companion, and so agreeable and well-bred, that she could not refuse. And I danced with our friend from La Turbie, and we often passed them on the floor, and they waved and nodded reassuringly. And the next dance was the blues. I took my partner back to her seat, but Cousin Rachel and her Frenchman kept right on.

And while the other people danced, I had leisure to take in the scene, and appreciate its points. At first I was conscious only of the general effect, the play of light and color, the welter of the dance, the shrieking, whistling, whinnying throng of men and women. And then I began to note details. The fat woman with the red coral ornaments was powdering her nose and strug-

gling vaguely with the paper balls that had got
lodged in the back of her dress. There was a
tennis-playing English girl in a red gown who
was athletically pelting everybody within range.
There was an elegant Englishman who gazed out
upon the world from behind his frosted eyeglass
with a vacant, genial, questioning, imperturbable stare. Here and there were bald-headed
men, solid in their seats, meditatively balancing
champagne bottles. It was in vain trying to determine the social status of the persons present,
they were all so mixed up together in the indul-
gent democracy of noise and merriment. Only
in general one might say that the fat and tired
and flashy people were of the better sort.

And the next dance was the blues, and still
my cousin Rachel kept on with her pleasant
Frenchman. There is something very seductive
about this dance, so suave and sleepy, swaying
and hesitating, cradle-rocking to the siren notes
of the saxophone; with the lights turned low, and
only here and there a shoulder gleaming in the
pink underseas glow. And very far away they
seemed, this swaying mass of men and women,
bathed in melancholy sentiment; cynical men

and women, returning with one accord to the dreams of adolescence. Now and then I caught sight of my Englishman, swimming into view behind his frosty monocle, treading the measure solemnly in the arms of some lithe female, grinning, fatuous, moving mechanically, silent, happy; through the yellow light, the green light, the pink light, led in a trance.

By this time it was past midnight, and our friends from La Turbie had taken their leave. Rachel said we would only stay for half an hour. But now her partner suggested that he should take us over to the Carlton. He was, it seems, a French lawyer, who had retired from business, and had chosen Monte Carlo as the place where one might best live a life of refined pleasure. It was hard for strangers, he said, to know where to go. After midnight the Carlton was decidedly the place that had the most *chic*. Shouldn't we like to step over there for half an hour and open a bottle of champagne?

I was loth to accept this invitation. I thought of Edward Junior slaving away at Williams, and of Edward Senior at the office in South Bend. I was rather tired myself. And I had a vague notion that we oughtn't to put ourselves under obligation to this stranger, however agreeable he might be. I didn't know how long this half-hour might last, nor how many bottles of champagne might logically be involved, nor what other social complications might arise in the course of the evening. I didn't know just what this French lawyer fancied he was making by his friendliness, what "reasonable expectation" he might base on our acceptance. But Rachel was evidently bent on going. She always welcomed an occasion for extending her knowledge of French. It never occurred to her that the privilege of talking to her might not be sufficient return for any trouble one might put himself to on her account. Her *avocat* was an excellent dancer. And to tell the truth, I suppose the champagne already consumed may have operated to give an attraction to the champagne in prospect.

And so we floated over, amid the soft lights and palms of this caressing February night. The Carlton proved to be a pretty place indeed, with its still more intimate dancing-floor, its galleries hung with flowers, its little tables set out with shaded lamps and bottles in silver coolers. The

company was more select than that of the Café
de Paris. There were none of those skinny, tennis-playing English girls, and no fat women
shaking paper balls out of the backs of their
dresses. Every table had its fresh and pretty girl
in a Paris frock. Our *avocat* ordered champagne
of the best mark, and set out with little delay to
find dancing partners for me. I said I didn't
want to put him to any trouble, but he said they
were all playmates of his, and he landed me at a
table with, I am frank to say, two of the most
delicious creatures I have encountered in my
travels. I was evidently to make my choice.
They were, he explained, dancers at the Opera.
And they certainly were adepts at the tango and
the fox trot. One of them was a Titian blonde
in a slinky orange velvet gown. She was recently from her native Milan, and knew even
less French than I, and no English at all. But
she had speaking eyes.

The other was a little, dreamy woman in a
green panniered confection out of Watteau. She
was very fond of American music, and was engaged in learning the words of our popular song,
"My Only One." I was able to give her some

help in framing those difficult syllables. The song had been brought to her attention by an American friend to whom she presented me. He was a graduate of Dartmouth College who was evidently on intimate terms with the proprietor, and seemed to be generally well at home at the Carlton. It seems that he had pull in the musical world, and he hoped to get a Chicago engagement for our little friend. Our little friend had more wit than the occasion really called for, and her wisdom quite took my breath away. I don't know how the talk turned to philosophy, but I thought perhaps that was too big a word for her, and I asked her if she knew what philosophy was. "Oh, yes," she said, she thought she did. "Wasn't philosophy the art of living without thought?"

That seemed to me a very good definition, and I ordered champagne and oranges for the Watteau philosopher, and gave myself over to a thoughtless enjoyment of the occasion. Rachel and her *avocat* were installed behind a sort of pillar where I couldn't see much of them, but I got an impression that they were getting along very nicely, and when we passed them on the dancing floor, they seemed to be the best of friends. Cousin Rachel smiled indulgently upon my little idyl; but I don't think she took into account any temptations to which I might be exposed. She was getting an unusually good lesson in French.

The Englishman with the frosted eyeglass turned up, walking steadily, dancing gravely, and sitting tight, with the look of a dazed but imperturbable satyr. There was an American matron in cream-colored satin who was taking lessons in the tango from a swarthy looking man who spoke French with an Italian rasp. At one table were two young American men busily imbibing champagne with the help of two young women of the house. One of them would occasionally break out in a little fit of yodeling, to the great delight of his companion, who informed us in a loud whisper, "You see he has *bean* to Switzerland, he has *bean* to Switzerland!" There were some very good Spanish dancers who were good mimics too, and they gave an exhibition of a lovers' quarrel and reconciliation which was quite killing. One of the girls, who perhaps had had too much, went into hysterics over this, and then she tried to carry away the male dancer, and there was a furious quarrel with the female Spaniard; and the American who had been to Switzerland tried to interfere, and quite a rumpus ensued. There was another girl, who really didn't belong at the Carlton, for she was, to tell the truth, a little flyblown. She did not think her "friend" was giving her enough attention— for he was flirting with the Titian blonde in orange velvet—and she began to cry, and the proprietor came up and said he'd have to put her out, and she said she didn't care, she'd leave Monte Carlo, and she'd never come back, it was no place for a decent, self-respecting girl. And the proprietor soothed her down, and straightened her hair, and introduced her to the monocled Englishman, and she wiped her eyes and began to dance, and soon she was laughing gaily; and as for the Englishman, he wiped his eyeglass, and he went through the measure like a well-bred satyr.

At half-past two I joined Rachel and her *avocat* for a moment, and made a faint suggestion that we might be going home. But Rachel didn't seem to be in a hurry, and the *avocat* inquired if I wasn't pleased with my little friend. I said yes, she was certainly charming. And he said to Rachel: "You see, he is well suited. We'll see no more of him tonight." Well, I thought Rachel was entitled to all the fun she could get, and I went back to my little friend.

At three o'clock Rachel came up, rather red in the face and somewhat out of breath, and said we'd better be going home now. She was followed by her *avocat*, looking baffled and bewildered, but always polite. I hurried Rachel to the cloakroom, and then came back to settle for the champagne. My last hundred-franc note I disposed of to my Watteau philosopher, asking her to get herself some little memento of the occasion. She, too, seemed bewildered, and wanted to know if I had made my arrangements with the orange velvet. I said no, I had to take my cousin back to the hotel. "*Alors, ça ne va pas?*" said she, meaning that my cousin hadn't hit it off with her *avocat*. I looked blank, and she looked bewildered. By this time the *avocat* had consoled himself with the orange velvet. He was evidently in a state of nervous excitement, and he had a sort of glazed look behind his *pince-nez*.

I went to join Rachel in the cloakroom, but I lingered a moment at the door while the Watteau philosopher tried to explain things to the proprietor. She seemed to think their *avocat* had been badly treated, but the proprietor only shrugged his shoulders. He had long since given up trying to understand the American point of view.

As we walked back to the hotel, I got from Rachel a rather vague account of things. It seems the Frenchman had taken *au sérieux* the advances she had made, and when we accepted his invitation to the Carlton, he must have concluded that everything was arranged, especially after he got me so nicely settled with our little friend. As the evening wore on, he kept trying to hold Rachel's hand, and he was always telling her they wouldn't see anything more of me, and they might as well take to the woods. I don't think he took much stock in our cousinship. She found it amusing in the earlier stages—she was having a very good French lesson—but as he got more insistent she grew frightened and made a break.

I was somewhat troubled by what I had overheard between the proprietor and my little friend. I had the feeling that we had somehow failed to meet some obligation; we had broken the rules of some game with which we were not familiar. Was there a point of view from which it might be said that we had not played fair with Rachel's *avocat*? But I said nothing of this to Rachel. She was satisfied that she had come off on the whole very creditably from the affair. And she was pleased to have such unmistakable evidence of the depravity of the Latin man.

DANCING PARTNERS AND
DANCING MASTERS

III

DANCING PARTNERS AND DANCING MASTERS

T HE first time that we saw Apollo in the flesh was at the municipal casino in Nice at the hour of the afternoon "dancing." I recognized him at once by his superb figure, his London tailor, his well-waved and well-brushed chestnut hair, his perfect breeding, and the cool glance out of his well-set gray eyes. He was as perfect as if he had been picked a trifle unripe from the tree in Oregon, carefully wrapped in stamped paper, and shipped directly to the consumer. I must say at once that Aspasia did not agree with me in my identification of him with Apollo. To her he seemed to be a particularly uninteresting young American, who showed no evidence of thought or suffering, or of the possession of any ideal other than that of social correctness. But Aspasia, as I have often observed to her, is not particularly discriminating in masculine beauty, and she does not appreciate the peculiar rare charm of a certain polished immaturity. When he took the floor to dance with his mother, she had to acknowledge that he carried himself well and that he was an excellent dancer. His mother was herself a handsome woman, almost as tall as her son, and with a figure admirably preserved.

The casino at Nice is one of those favored places where they can manage to put on a tango now and then without emptying the floor of dancers. We had recently received some instruction in the intricacies of that difficult and seemingly simple dance and the proper form to be observed in moving through its steps. And we recognized this couple as quite the best on the floor, moving with stately grace and ease where most dancers seem to be falling over their feet. It was a pleasure to watch them, and I certainly was sorry to see them go at the end of the third or fourth dance. They were evidently people of the first society, whether of Kansas City or New York, and had presumably other appointments which made it impossible to linger very long in a place which, after all, is open to the general public. Their appearances were always brief and meteoric, whether at the Negresco, or the Ruhl at the

thé dansant, or at the Carlton in Monte Carlo after the opera. For we came upon them often after
that; they were evidently dancing their way
through Europe. At the Carlton, they arrived at
the correct moment, a quarter to one, and left at
the discreet moment of quarter past two. They
were magnificent specimens of what we can do in
the way of *haut ton* when we set ourselves to it,
and such as we were content to have exhibited
for the admiration of the world.

This proved to be a characteristic feature of
the foreign landscape: the American woman of
middle age traveling in Europe with her son,
while the father remains at home to look after
the business. But we were not always so well
satisfied with the specimens presented to European observation. It was in Naples that we found
ourselves on a footing of something almost like
intimacy with such a couple, owing to the circumstance of our having been at the same pension in
Rome. They were people, this time, of our own
social level, from Riverside, California, where the
father was engaged in the practice of the law.
They were very nice people, both of them, greatly admired by the English boarders, but it was

the son whom we were inclined to favor. He was a tall, modest, pink-cheeked young man, with a high-pitched voice, and a kind of suppressed eagerness for life. He was just out of high school, and had not yet determined where to go to college, or what career to choose for himself. His great passion was for the stage. But Europe did not do much to feed this flame. He wanted to go to Vienna on account of the theater, but his mother was afraid to venture so far into the enemy's country; and, to tell the truth, they were ill prepared for the dramatic art of Vienna, with not more than five German words between them. Very touching was the eagerness with which he received our suggestions in regard to theaters in Paris; and his gratitude became positively lyric when we informed him that, in the very pension where we were putting up, there was a New York man engaged in producing a film for Griffith and the Gishes. He was determined at once to secure an interview with so notable a personage.

This young Roscius was obviously ill at ease under the jealous tutelage of his mother, and indeed it is possible to conceive of how one might with greater wisdom fulfil the office of maternal guardian. It was humiliating to witness the strictness with which she exercised her function, the way she dealt out five-lira notes to him for the purchase of chocolate, and supervised his potations. She might herself drink two or three glasses of light wine, at a picnic luncheon, because she was thirsty and there was no water to be had; but however thirsty he might be, he must confine himself to one small glass because he was still young and liable to form habits. In all her attitude toward him there was a curious mingling of the anxious mother and the jaunty companion. No doubt she was making a valiant effort to keep young for his sake, to present an appearance like that of Apollo's mother. To see her at dinner, with her long earrings and carefully dressed hair, and, I suppose, a touch of artificial color, you might suppose that she had really preserved the freshness of youth. But she was in point of fact a nervous invalid, incapable of taking the pace demanded by his years, and yet not reconciled to letting him out of her sight.

We were not the only ones who had felt the pity of the situation. She had had a disagreement, as she confided to us, with American

friends with whom they were traveling. The
friends had been inclined to interfere and even to
encourage the son in his petty efforts at self-
emancipation. We could not but agree that a
mother must be the best judge of how to treat
her own son, and that it is other people's business
to fall in with her system, or else to clear out. We
cleared out ourselves as soon as we became aware
of the final humiliation she put upon her eight-
een-year-old son: that of occupying one room
with her at the hotel! The innocence of American
manners is proverbial with Europeans, and their
landlords are accustomed to receive with *sang-
froid* the most surprising manifestations of eccen-
tricity. But I doubt if they have ever been given
a more astounding instance of our peculiar ways
of regarding things.

Young Roscius made no bones about his desire to get his mother off his hands. But his will
had been so long systematically starved that he
was incapable of asserting himself. He thought
he would like to attend some European university during the coming year. And we did our best
for him by suggesting to his mother that Geneva
has an excellent university, and is a place where

one could leave one's son with a minimum of risk
to his morals. And the last that we heard was
that she is seriously considering taking a flat in
the Swiss Paris with a view to supervising the
studies of her son!

This mother, with her queer, bewildered
brain, is a subject for psychologists more expert
than I. They would probably conclude that ego-
ism plays as great a part as sense of duty in the
extreme jealousy with which she regards her fil-
ial charge. They would perhaps suggest that her
love for her son is in part an unconscious substi-
tute for the love which no longer prevails between her and the husband who practices law in
Riverside.

These partial substitutions are seemingly not
uncommon in a world where the men attend to
business and the women turn their attention to
the arts. And the pleasure cities of Europe make
suitable provision for the needs of American
women in this kind. There is a curious institution along the Riviera which seems to be specially organized for the benefit of American ladies
with time on their hands. At the casinos of Nice
and Monte Carlo, and at the great hotels in those

cities, you are surprised to note the large number
of slender, correct, young men in black suits and
with black hair neatly plastered down, who make
a point, at tea time, of offering themselves as
dancing partners to the stout American ladies
who mostly frequent those resorts. Nothing can
exceed the propriety of these gentlemen, the tired,
sober worldliness, even the boredom, of their de-
portment. If the lady is accompanied by a gentleman who does not dance, they will, of course,
make application to the gentleman himself, in-
quiring in most polite, if technical, terms whether he would like to have him take the lady for a
dance: *"Voulez-vous que je fasse danser Madame?"* They are accomplished dancers, and
nothing more could be wished in the way of
partners. Only, they all look alike, and they are,
when you come to find out—well, they are professionals. They are for hire!

Nothing is said about this aspect of the matter, but an understanding prevails among the in-
itiated that, on leaving the tearoom, the lady, or
her husband, shall slip a bill in the hand of the
obliging young man. There is even something
like a tariff, on which you may consult any of the

functionaries of the hotel. I have known a man
to give fifty francs to one of these professionals
for dancing once with his wife. That was perhaps
a bit ostentatious. But in that case, to tell the
truth, it was fifty francs well earned.

I don't know how society could be maintained
on the Riviera if it were not for these volunteers.
The lady who has spent her morning in the sump-
tuous establishments of the Boulevard Masséna
has little to do in the afternoon but wear to tea
the gowns which she has so carefully chosen. If
her husband has come abroad with her, he will
doubtless be good enough to accompany her to
tea, but he will draw the line at dancing. He enjoys the sunshine on the Riviera, and the *New
York Herald*, the cocktails, and an occasional trial
of fortune on the wheel. He likes to watch the
dancing, and the solo dances under the spotlight
are put on for his particular benefit. He enjoys
those feats of suppleness of the latest danseuse
from New York or Barcelona! But for the more
aesthetic side of life, he leaves that to his wife
and daughters. He is probably a little older than
his wife. At any rate he has sooner become reconciled to the placid outlook of middle age.

And it has always been notoriously hard to find men suitable to the purposes of society. These well-to-do American ladies are naturally somewhat exigent in their demands. They cannot go to the more common places where dancing partners are more abundant. They cannot take up with men who may prove in the end to be a social handicap. They must consider the claims of their position. *Noblesse oblige.* But they cannot quite reconcile themselves to going without men for the whole period of their European sojourn. And here are these most presentable persons ready to step into the breach. They understand the new dances quite as well as you do. They have, naturally, a command of the French language, in itself a mark of refinement. They make no claims for consideration beyond the moment. They are always respectful in manner. If they do have a little the air of being dissipated, that is often the case with young men in the best society at home. And they never start a flirtation unless plainly invited to do so. And so the emotional needs of the women are served at the same time that numerous deserving young men manage to earn a living.

It is not the occupation which I should recommend for a young man ambitious to make a career. But there are openings everywhere to an enterprise that partakes of the nature of genius. There is one man in Nice who seems to be making a very good thing of this occupation of professional partner combined with that of dancing master. But M. Montero is not alone in this undertaking, and he owes it largely to the vision and the practical sense of Mme Montero that their affairs are prospering so well, and that they follow a busy winter season at Nice with an equally busy summer season at Aix-les-Bains. It is advisedly that I use the word "vision" in connection with the work of Mme Montero. It was this which led her originally to see the possibilities of M. Montero as a dancing master at a time when he was only a disabled matador, which supported her in the years in which she nursed him back to health from the wound of the bull, and through the still more difficult years of getting a start in their profession.

The dominant note in the art, as in the manners, of the Monteros is decorum. M. Montero is not at first glance a very prepossessing figure:

short of stature, and with a bad eye, memento of his bull-fighting days. But he has a certain grave, sweet dignity which immediately distinguishes him from the riffraff of the dance halls. He carries himself as well in his neat blue serge or his close-cut "smoking" as if he were dressed out in all the splendor of the toreador. He is as strong as a bull, and as shapely as Antinous. He is a man of fire and bronze. He holds his partner with the firmness necessary to control her every movement, but with no hint of vulgarity. He "moves like a wave of the sea." He is master of the long, straight-legged stride that is the key to good form in all the modern dances. And he has a perfect instinct for the nuances of rhythm and movement that make the individual distinction of the tango, the *paso doble*, the Boston, and the fox-trot.

When I first entered the anteroom of their little academy, I confess that I was amused at the framed certificates of their proficiency in the art of dancing which adorned the walls. There were individual diplomas for the *Championnat du monde des danses* at Paris, and a joint diploma from the Bal Tabarin certifying to their winning the prize in the *Concours de tango*. It was simply my ignorance that made me smile. I had no notion of the talent and the discipline, of the taste and the intelligence, implied in these achievements. I had no notion of this strenuous art which is the last word of sensuousness and law in a happy union. But the Monteros opened my eyes.

Above all, they impressed me with the sincerity and refinement of their ideal. When we met them at the Negresco it was natural to discuss the dancing of those on the floor. We came to share the critical spirit with which they regarded certain dancers, most often Americans, who made of the dance a kind of gymnastic exercise, and seemed to enjoy themselves in proportion to the violence of the contortions through which they went. The Monteros had no patience with anything vulgar or flashy in the dance, with what they called the "negro style." When Aspasia pointed out that some of the dances were, in origin, negro art, Mme Montero agreed. They came from America, North or South, and they brought with them some of the high color, some of the unregulated vivacity of their primitive origin. But then the French taste began to work upon them; they were refined and brought within bounds; and so they became the truly beautiful forms we perceive in the handling of competent artists, who realize that energy is all the more effective for being directed. Unfortunately, every boat brought a horde of young barbarians with untamed energies flowering in manifold variety of the bizarre and the outlandish. And all too few of them had the grace to submit themselves to the disciplinary instruction of the Monteros!

The Monteros gave us little hope of finding the true gospel of the dance outside of France. In Italy, they assured us, there was no comprehension of the art, and they could not recommend us to any qualified masters there. It was by sheer accident that we found our way to the academy of Professor Nenni, whose traffic is almost exclusively with Roman youths and maidens who hope to make themselves presentable in a social way. It is true that they have a palace in which to practice their steps, as so often in Italy the most humble trades are carried on in places reminiscent of patrician splendor, machinists driving their smutty, ear-splitting business behind marble balconies and Venetian-Gothic windows. So Professor Nenni was installed in a suite of rooms including a salon of the *seicento*, with patterned marble floor, with gold chairs and pillared walls, and statues of the gods, and a green marble bowl of goldfish, and with a ceiling painted by a world-famous painter with vine-trellis and cupids. And there, upon that floor and beneath that fictive heaven, the members of the Sunday Club, with pursed lips and wrinkled brows, go through the one-two and the one-two-three of the dances they are learning.

It was by recommendation of Professor Nenni that we visited in Florence the celebrated academy of Landolina in the Via della Vigna Nuova. We did not test the quality of Landolina as a dancing master, but we made out well enough why his fame should have reached all the way to Rome. It was not so obviously a palace in which he held his sessions, but the characteristic feature was the tables lining the walls, with their bright-colored china and glassware. For the costs of the entertainment were here defrayed by the charge for afternoon tea or supper. It was here that Italian gentlemen took tea *à l'anglaise*, and English ladies took cocktails *à l'américaine*. Landolina had an orchestra that played excellent jazz, at least for Italy. And his rooms were open every afternoon of the week and every evening except Wednesday. He had hit upon something better than the business of a teacher. It was not a dancing-school that he conducted, but a dance hall, which is one variety of café, and, in our frivolous day, the most paying variety. Long live Landolina! And Professor Nenni take notice. The business of the dancing teacher may have declined since the time of the armistice, but the art of dancing still flourishes lustily.

I know not how it should ever cease to flourish, being, as it is, so pure an expression of our will to live, our affirmation of beauty. There is nothing utilitarian about the dance. It has no reference to any good beyond itself; and it has its points of superiority over every other variety of aesthetic enjoyment. There is something passive and incomplete about the contemplation of painting and sculpture. Music is to be enjoyed thoroughly only by the composer in the act of creation, or perhaps by the performer in the act of rendering; it is only with them that the whole organism enters into the aesthetic experience. And it is only in the dance that one gives thorough employment to this body of ours, this minister of beauty. Tennis is good fun, but tennis is a game, and the passion for beating someone comes in to vitiate the aesthetic character of our pleasure. In sport we divide our homage; in dancing we worship but the one god.

It is a pity that dancing is so often degraded by the intrusion of extraneous considerations, social and humanitarian: must I propitiate this powerful lady by inviting her to dance? Should I take pity on this fading wallflower and stick her in my buttonhole? Nothing should be allowed to interfere with the choice of partners on purely aesthetic grounds. I care not for your social standing. I care not what you may have in your head. I pick you for your lightness of foot, your suppleness, your instinct for rhythm. You are a priestess of beauty, and your personality enters not at all into your vestal office except in so far as it may serve the goddess.

It is not to the Negresco that one should go for the spirit of the dance, nor the palatial casino at Monte Carlo. It is to some commoner place, where there is less consciousness of style and rank, and a purer devotion to the art. I favor the jetty promenade at Nice. The society is mixed, no doubt, corresponding to the moderate price of the *consommations*, and the dancers are at every stage of expertness. It is like a dance hall at Long Beach by the Pacific. But this very lowering of the standard admits many young people who do most honor the dance. There is the long-haired youth in a spotty coat and baggy trousers who is always to be seen at the jetty of an afternoon. He is some student or otherwise ill-furnished person, but he is a beautiful dancer, and there is no girl who is not glad to get him for a partner. Is it the bushy-haired Nicaraguan in a green sweater who is such an adept at the *paso doble?* Is it the svelte girl in a tailored suit, with her little boy's head in her straight bobbed hair, whose long legs hold the secret of the tango and the Boston? He takes them in turn and puts them through their paces. He takes the dance seriously and he goes through it with a kind of sacred joy. For the dance is, at bottom, a religious exercise. It is a reconciliation of man with nature. It is here that he forgets his unhappy separation from the rest of the universe, the act of thought and will by which he sets himself over against the unconscious. And the light that lightens his countenance is the testimony to the satisfaction of one who moves with the stars in their courses.

> And with joy the stars perform their shining,
> And the sea its long, moon-silver'd roll.

The afternoon is the best time at the jetty. For in the evening they put up the artificial barrier of the dinner coat, and our student is not admitted. One of our American friends had an amusing experience with this regulation. He is a young man fond of dancing, and he had strolled into the jetty dance hall after dinner in hopes of finding a partner. But after sitting down at a table and ordering coffee, he became aware of a printed notice, in which, so far as he could make out, it was required of all gentlemen in the evening to smoke tobacco: *Après sept heures du soir,* he read, *le smoking est obligatoire.* Now our friend is one of those men who do not like tobacco, and at any rate it seemed to him a fantastic reversal of the American custom of forbidding the use of tobacco in places frequented by women. Personally, he thought it should be left to the free choice of every gentleman whether or not he should seek the solace of the weed. This was, perhaps, he considered, another instance of European petty graft. It was their way of making you pay for your entertainment. You have to purchase a package of cigarets as you have to order something to drink. When the waiter came with his coffee, he summoned up courage to inquire the meaning of the strange sign.

"Is it true," he asked, "that smoking is required of all gentlemen?"

"Why, yes," said the waiter, "it is required of all gentlemen who desire to dance. If you do not wish to dance, it makes no difference."

That but served to puzzle him the more. It seemed peculiar that one might sit at one's table alone without smoking, but that as soon as one stepped on the floor with a lady one must light a cigar. And besides, he could not observe that any of the dancers were actually smoking.

"But look here!" he exclaimed to the waiter, "I can't see anybody smoking on the floor."

And then the waiter put the case more plainly. In the evening, he explained, gentlemen who wished to dance were expected to wear evening dress. And so our friend learned that there was more than a box of cigarets involved. He would be debarred from dancing after dinner on the jetty until his trunk arrived from Paris.

This may be all very well as a move in the game of social exclusion, but it clearly has nothing to do with the fine art of the dance.

INTERNATIONAL

IV

INTERNATIONAL

O F ALL things I love to spend a day in a second-class compartment on a European railway. The compartment is a much more sociable division of space than the double seat in one of our Pullmans. It accommodates more people, and throws them together in much greater privacy—a sort of common privacy, to be sure, which compels a more intimate relation than we should be likely to develop on our own initiative. There we are, shut in from the world, moving swiftly through space, skirting the shores of seas, tunneling mountains, leaving behind strange cities. Nothing outside our little cell has more than a notional existence. Night and day are all one, and storm and bright weather. We are subject to no locality save that of our own creation. Tomorrow we shall go our several ways, and become parts of Ferrara, Padua, or Venice. Today we constitute a city and a society of our own.

I do not care so much for this situation when we are compatriots, or even when we speak the same language. It is not to make observations upon ourselves that we travel in Europe, nor to associate with ourselves. We know ourselves but too well, and are eager to escape, for the period of our holiday, into a region of psychology more romantic and less familiar. We Americans in particular are all trying to escape one another, but alas! Europe is not big enough; nor Africa, for that matter. Tunis and Algiers are full of us and our kodaks, and Biskra knoweth the honk of our motor horns.

I have in mind an August afternoon going from Milan to Brieg, passing the enchanted shores of Lago Maggiore. I was the only occupant of the compartment who was not a member of the Dexter Tours, a concern operating in the states of Kentucky and Tennessee, and drawing its recruits exclusively from a sect of Christians who base their doctrine on a special interpretation of a verse in the Book of Daniel. Dr. Dexter was a lively and efficient young man, who circulated industriously among the members of the party and did his best to cheer them up with his stock of jokes and anecdotes and merry quips. And he had need of all his gaiety. The party was made up largely of nervous elderly folk, rather exhausted with their task of keeping up to their schedule, and inclined to "lie down on the job" of sight-seeing. I knew these people as well as if I had been brought up with them and attended the same Sunday school and Christian Endeavor Society. They were primarily good people, worn out by the strain of doing their duty and starving their instincts.

Miss Amanda was the one I liked the best. She had evidently looked forward for the length of her life to this bath of culture and beauty. She had been a school teacher, I imagine, or had borne the brunt of bringing up someone else's children. She sat very quiet, with her poor stringy hands crossed in her lap, and gazed wistfully out of the window, and the vines and mulberry trees and campaniles brightened her eyes with something like the beatific vision.

Stout Mr. Penguin showed no interest in anything but his stomach. Not that he complained; he was much too good a Christian for that. But his very silence was eloquent, and

Mrs. Penguin at regular intervals made sympathetic inquiry after the state of his feelings. He always contended that he was much better, or was about to be so. Mrs. Penguin was worried over his having had nothing to eat all day. As for Dr. Dexter, he kept popping in and out to make his inquiries, to crack a joke, or to urge on Mr. Penguin a finger of brandy. He had got out especially at a station to procure a flask of a very special variety. But Mr. Penguin, it seems, was a teetotaler, and he only shook his head. He was supported by his wife in his determination not to take a drop of brandy. "It would be the first time," she said.

"This is a very special brandy," said Dr. Dexter, "and very good for the stomach."

"It would be the first time," said Mrs. Penguin.

"It wouldn't hurt a child," said Dr. Dexter.

"It would be the first time," said Mrs. Penguin.

Her own recommendation in the circumstances was camphor, and Mr. Penguin agreed to try that remedy. It would be better with a lump of sugar, said Mrs. Penguin, and Mr. Penguin agreed. So the drinking cup was got out, and the camphor bottle, and Mr. Penguin had his two fingers of camphor with a lump of sugar. And everyone sank back exhausted from his exertions. It was a hot afternoon.

I could not see that Mr. Penguin was any the better for his camphor, and I felt rather depressed with all this sickroom business. I made my escape into the corridor, lowered the window, and settled down to the enjoyment of the scenery. We were now passing by the villas of the lake shore, with glimpses of the terraced islands, and the dusky mountainous shore beyond, sown with villages that caught the pink glow of the sunset. Young Miss Cynthia was watching the scenery at the next window, and she was like an advertisement of Coca Cola. I was not ill content when she began to talk. The lake, she said, reminded her of Love Lake in Tennessee, where they used to go for picnics. She wanted to know where I came from, and what business I was in, and where I had been in Italy. They had just come from Milan, where they had seen the cathedral and "The Last Supper," by Murillo. And the day before they were in Florence. There were some nice stores there, and they had visited the mission of their sect established at Florence for the conversion of the Italians. It was a mission supported largely by the churches in Tennessee, and the incumbent had been very kind to them and shown them all about the place. He said they had a considerable following in Florence, and were thinking of extending their operations to Rome. At this point in our discussion Dr. Dexter intervened with some jocular observation, and I returned to the compartment.

Mr. Penguin seemed rather better, but now it was Mrs. Penguin who had succumbed. It seems that all along she had been suffering from a severe headache, but had borne up bravely. At the moment that I entered she gave up the fight. With the help of Miss Amanda and Mr. Penguin she removed her shoes and otherwise disposed herself for a reclining position across the length of the seat. Miss Amanda took her head in her lap, and covered her eyes with a handkerchief dipped in camphor. It was not without a struggle that she yielded to her weakness, and she was now all in tears at the thought of the trouble she was giving. "It is nothing but a nervous headache," she kept saying. And everybody spoke to her in soothing voices, and agreed that it was only a nervous headache, but that she must lie quiet, and the journey had been a hard one. "You must try to get a little rest," said Mr. Penguin, sympathetically regarding her stockinged feet, and Miss Amanda sat patiently with her head in her lap, murmuring something in a sickroom tone of voice.

No, decidedly, it is foreigners that I prefer to find in my compartment. They offer more to the imagination, more to the speculative faculty, more to gratify our propensity for observation and research. What a favorable occasion for the philosopher in racial psychology! Here we are shut in together, free from all disturbance. We are a little cross-section of humanity mounted on a slide, strangely magnified by this proximity, and presented to the licensed curiosity of one another. We may sit at our ease and watch one another and try to understand the indications of dress and physiognomy and manner. We may arrive at a better understanding of our common humanity, or we may surprise some intimate secret of racial difference. It is surely no crime to listen to a conversation in a foreign language of which you do not catch one word in twenty, nor to make your profit of the few words you do catch to nourish your speculations on the mystery of race.

I have stretched my ears for an hour at a time only to catch the one remark: *"Mais que voulez-vous? Il y a des gens comme ça!"* (But what would you have? there are people like that.) And I felt amply rewarded for my attention. I did not know what sort of people they were speaking of, nor what absurdities or brutalities of such people had been recounted. But I knew what tone of voice was used in speaking of them, what attitude was taken, and I had wherewith to occupy me for a second hour, and build a pretty theory of the Gallic temperament. Those were not words at random. Those words I heard because I had heard them before, because I had met them so often in comedies and taken them straight from the lips of landladies and saleswomen. I may have made some mildly protesting inquiry as to the price of some article, thinking vaguely that I might thereby secure a reduction. *"Mais que voulez-vous, Monsieur?"* with a little shrug of the shoulders, and there follows a rapid survey of economic conditions affecting the cost of living, in a manner colored in equal parts with irony and with philosophical resignation. Or I may have been recounting to the landlady our troubles at the Odéon, where by great effort we arrived on time for the rising of the curtain only to have the first act of *Le Marchand de Venise* spoiled by the people who had come late crowding past our knees and hunting for a purse which one of them had dropped. *"Mais que voulez-vous?"* says Madame. One ought not to admit people who come late. But if the theaters followed that principle they would have no audiences. People like to eat their dinners at leisure. No plays ought to begin before nine o'clock.

"But then," I plead, "we should never get home before one."

"Voilà!" says Madame. *"Vous avez raison, Monsieur. Mais que voulez-vous?"*

It is the last word of a race that will not demand too much of life; it was not yesterday they learned that this is not the best of all possible worlds. They will aim at practicable ends; if they cannot have the whole cake, they will e'en content them with a slice. To the anomalies and contretemps of life they will oppose a humorous patience; if life is unreasonable, they at least will be reasonable; if life is *triste*, they will brighten it up with a touch of irony.

And when it comes to human nature, they will bring the comic spirit to play, with its infinite variety. In human nature nothing surprises them. For the vulgarities of foreigners they have the largest indulgence. They have so long watched the metro deposit at Rue Vavin the affectations and the sincerities of all nations! I have never known a Frenchman to be a snob. They understand too well the common motives of human action; they understand themselves too well. It is not that they have no pride of family or wealth. They have it more intensely, I fancy, than any curate's daughter or any Colonial Dame. At bottom they may be more firmly intrenched in their exclusiveness. But they are too good philosophers, too good psychologists, they have read history too well, to suppose that they have what they possess by divine right, or that it is to be counted to them for personal merit. They are glad enough of whatever advantage they possess in the game of social privilege, and at all costs they will hold on to it. But they do not imagine that they are the superiors of Anatole France, or Edison, or Hugo Stinnes! They have their standards in speech and manners. Their Paris is an academy specially constituted for laying down the law on these subjects. Their stage is the most conservative, the most hidebound. They know perfectly what is correct, what is admirable. But they are prepared to envisage without consternation every sort of variation from their norm. They do not cry out against the iniquity of people who differ from themselves. They enjoy them hugely; they tell stories about them; they present them in pantomime. But the limit of commentary in the way of judgment is a shrug of the shoulders: "But what would you have? There are people like that!"

Perhaps the gentle reader will think that I make too much of a few simple words, and that I might have heard something more exciting for all my trouble. But what will he say to the words that passed between the lady who got on at Mantua and the gentleman who got on at Verona? It is very seldom that the tourist has even a glimpse of really high-class people, above all in Italy. Really high-class Italians do not spend their time in second-class railway carriages between Milan and Venice. But this was a real lady by every indication. And the handsome young man who got on at Verona revealed the gentleman in every detail of his simple elegance. He immediately attracted the attention of the lady from Mantua, not because of his elegance, but because of something familiar in his appearance; and at last she broke out with the question whether he were not So-and-so, her husband's friend? Yes, he granted, with politeness but without effusion, he was So-and-so. And how was his wounded arm? Oh, that was entirely well now, he said, with a little smile of deprecation; it was never anything to speak of. Her husband had told her about the duel, she said, but she did not know much about his adversary. And so the young man was led to tell her about the duel and about his adversary. He was not the least bit excited, and he did not call his adversary a villain; the latter was not really a bad sort, it seemed, but he did not have the correct political opinions.

And this was my first taste of Italy! And this was the gentleman from Verona! Verona and Mantua! Romeo and Juliet! Capulet and Montagu! Will you not grant that I had matter for reflection all the way to Venice? Had I not materials for constructing a picture of Italian society, which should be at least plausible, at least sufficient for the needs of the imagination? In Venice I found a memorial tablet to one Felice Cavallotti, "soldier, legislator, poet," who died, in 1898, "by wretched causes torn from greater promise." When I looked him up in the Encyclopedia Britannica, I found that he was a turbulent political leader, made popular by his thirty-three duels, and that he was killed in the last of these duels by an editor of opposed political views, "whom he had assailed with characteristic intemperance of language."

These dueling people are naturally too high-class to hold any communication with strangers in a railway carriage. But with more ordinary folks it will go hard but we shall scrape up some sort of acquaintance, spending our life together in this intimate way for a whole day perhaps. We are bound to make some exchange of courte-

sies at least, and that is the international exchange on which I set most store.

Everybody in Europe seems eager to demon-
strate a knowledge of English. It is generally
confined to the words "good night," and "all
right," but they go to the most absurd lengths to
drag in these magic syllables, their faces suffused
with a smile of infinite pride. It is not often that
they are sufficiently advanced in their knowledge of our language to ask discriminating questions. But there was, by exception, an Italian
officer who took advantage of our company on
the train to inform himself on several nice points
of idiom. He wanted to know, for example, what
one says on being thanked for a service rendered.
Someone had instructed him to reply, "Not at
all!"

"She say, 'You are very kind, I thank you!'"

"I say, 'Not at all!'"

It was a very important matter, affecting, as
it did, the forms of courtesy by which we class
ourselves socially. We had taken great pains to
learn to say in Italian, under similar circumstances, *Prego!* and in French, *Je vous en prie!*
But we were rather at a loss what to tell the in-

quiring officer. We Saxons have a natural dis-
inclination to these stereotyped forms, and such
as we have get vulgarized so soon! There must
be some more choice way of expressing the
deprecatory *prego!* But we could not for the life
of us think what it was. I couldn't even call to
mind that my mother had taught me to say,
"You are welcome!" We had no idea in what
company our lieutenant was planning to exercise his English; what sort of girl, from Boston
or Birmingham, he was accustomed to conduct
through the mazes of the fox-trot. On the whole,
we thought "not at all" would do very well; he
had been much better advised than if they had
told him to say, "Don't mention it!" And we
knew that he would go a long way on his kid
gloves and his smile.

It was a pretty Italian girl who loosened the
tongue of the officer and brought about these international *pourparlers*. And I take to myself
the credit of having secured her for our compartment. We were already five persons: two
English women and the lieutenant, besides Aspasia and me. And that is, Heaven knows,
enough for one compartment. But when she

got on at Pistoia with a large company of men and women, and they asked us point-blank whether there were any free places, it was I who piped up with the honesty of a George Washington and said there were exactly three places left.

Aspasia said nothing, but I could feel her stiffen in her seat beside me, and I knew what she thought of my gallantry. They were clearly not our sort of people. I say nothing of the horrid little peroxide with penciled eyes, who had smoked too many cigarets in her time, and who was evidently now in an advanced stage of tuberculosis. It was not for her that I was telling the truth. The others owed less to make-up, and were, indeed, very attractive specimens of womanhood, vivid brown-eyed beauties, the one in the bountifulness of motherhood, the other in the effervescence of youth. It was the mother who carried the dog, an intelligent little spaniel with a collar, who had his own special ticket. They at once began a lively conversation. They were, it seems, a theatrical company, touring the country in the English play, *Peg del mio Cuore*, "Peg o' My Heart," which they had recently put on at

Pistoia. The dog was one of the actors, and had his own rôle in the play.

They talked to one another and to the dog, but they were not unwilling that we should listen and take an interest. Especially the girl, whose remarks were often over the head of the dog. The lieutenant sat stiff in his corner with his gloves well buttoned. They were clearly not his sort of people. But he could not long hold out against the frank appeal of youth and high spirits. Before he knew it he had made friends with the dog and was in intimate converse with the girl. His gloves had come off, and he used them to emphasize his gestures. And before we were done, the conversation had become general; except, of course, for the English women, who didn't seem to be there. They were a much traveled company, these actors, having been three times to America to play. The mother acknowledged that it would have been more convenient if she had known three words of English. The daughter was bent on mastering such jaw-breakers as Cholmondeley and Algernon.

At one of the stops refreshments were had. The heroine of *Peg* was supplied with an orange, but she would not consume it all herself. She insisted on sharing it with her new friends. I was myself the recipient of one section, which I ate with extreme relish and with something of a sacramental feeling. They were not what we call high-class people, but it is the courtesies of low-class people that I rate the highest. It is only the poor who share, says Oscar Wilde. As for the English women, they judged things differently. One of them leaned over and asked me if I had ever been to the Zoo.

"The Zoo?" said I.

"Yes, the Zoo, in London, where they keep the animals."

Well, yes, I had been to the Zoo.

And didn't this remind me of the Zoo?

Alas, poor woman, she knew not what she said! And yet she meant well after all; this was her own feeble attempt at fraternization. She was not an absolute snob. But she thought she knew where to draw the line.

In Germany and Austria only six persons are admitted to one compartment, and the seats are conspicuously labeled, so that there is never any doubt as to the number of places occupied.

In Italy the quota of the compartment is eight persons, and the seats are not numbered. It is always very hard to know how many people have established themselves there; and, on the appearance of a newcomer, the occupants all with one accord begin to lie about it. And since it is impossible to reserve your places in advance, and they never have enough cars, the prudent traveler will come early, and for the timid traveler there is no place at all!

Aspasia and I arrived in good season at the train from Venice to Tarvisio; but this train had come on from Rome, and the compartments were all apparently full of people talking German. *Alles besetzt!* was the formula with which we were greeted at every door. In one compartment there seemed to be a slight vagueness in the declarations of the passengers. One seat was certainly unoccupied at the moment, and I told Aspasia to sit down there, while I addressed myself to finding another for me. On my third inquiry, the gentleman from Hungary yielded a point. He would make no claim to any seat but his own.

"*Hier bin ich!*" says he, and that's as far as he would go.

"*Also, hier bin ich!*" says I, throwing my hat down in the seat beside him. And I proceeded to stow as many of our bags as possible in the racks. There was such a mass of miscellaneous luggage there already that it was very hard to determine the exact state of the case. But in ten minutes we were thoroughly established, and amicably exchanging cigarets with the original occupants. There was the gentleman from Bohemia, and the gentleman from Hungary. They were returning from Sicily, where, they informed us slyly, they had been hunting snipe. There was a portly gentleman from Poland, who kept his gloves on, and whose language was German. There was a good-looking young man, likewise gloved, and whose nationality still remains in doubt, who never opened his mouth. And there was a well-groomed gentleman from Japan, who also held his silence, but who was industriously preparing himself for conversation in English, French, German, and Italian by the study of a phrase-book entitled *The Traveler in Europe*. That, together with Aspasia and me, makes seven passengers. But it was generally supposed in the compartment that there was still another man with a claim to a seat by the door, a man with a beard, who had established his residence by depositing some of his luggage in the racks overhead. Some of the passengers would occasionally leave their seats to stretch their legs in the corridor; so that it was very hard to make sure of the exact number.

But we were all agreed that the compartment was full.

And now occurred an incident which was a sore trial to the tempers of all persons concerned, and which threatened to become an international episode, entailing what the diplomats call "grave consequences." At a certain station there appeared in the corridor a blond lady in a cravenette traveling-coat, in the company of an Italian officer. She naturally wanted a seat, and she had appealed to the officer to find her a place in the midst of the Huns. It was a favorable moment, since the Polish gentleman was smoking a cigaret in the corridor, and the place beside his was also temporarily vacant. There was first a long consultation in the corridor, and then the officer put his head in to inquire what places were free. We all cried out that the compartment was entirely *occupato*. There followed another consultation between the officer and the lady, in which he was evidently coaching her in her part. He then introduced her into the compartment and told her to "sit there," indicating the seat of the Polish gentleman. *"Grazie, Capitano,"* said the blond lady graciously. She took her seat, and he bowed himself out.

The blond lady sits a bit stiffly in her seat and looks about her with assurance, as much as to say, What are you going to do about it? And none of my companions is moved to do anything about it. The Japanese gentleman is busy with *The Traveler in Europe,* and the others are evidently conscious of the officer just around the corner. Only the Polish gentleman stands helpless in the doorway and gazes upon the woman who has taken his seat.

Now I do not yield to anyone in my regard for the ladies, and the military and the clergy I always treat with the same distinguished consideration. But there is a question of justice involved here which transcends the claims of any of these privileged classes. And I am irresistibly impelled to inform this blond lady that in this compartment all the places are taken. I give her this information in my best Italian, and I am a bit nettled when she replies that she doesn't understand. She has evidently determined upon the policy of not understanding. On my repeating my explanation she replies again, more offensively,"*Il tedesco non l'intendo. Non mi piace.*" (I don't understand German. I don't care for that language.) I reply with some heat that I'm talking Italian: "*Non parlo tedesco. Parlo italiano.*" She then condescends so far as to say that there are evidently places free; there are eight places to each compartment, and here are only five persons. I proceed to count for her benefit: *uno*, the gentleman from Hungary; *due*, the gentleman from Bohemia; *tre*, my wife; *quattro*, myself; *cinque*, this gentleman with the kid gloves; *sei*, the Japanese gentleman; *sette*, the Polish gentleman (still looking through the door); *otto*, the gentleman with a beard, who has temporarily left his place.

The sole answer of the blond lady to this demonstrative argument is a sweeping gesture, and the words, "You see, there are but five persons."

None of my companions had said a word, and

it was evident that they were getting nervous.
They were thinking of the officer around the corner. There was not a German among them, but
they knew what is thought of persons speaking
the language of the Reich. As for myself, I had
no fear. I had my passport in my pocket. I was
a tribune of the people, and a teacher whose doctrine had been questioned by a recalcitrant pupil.

"Madam," I said, "there are already eight
persons in the compartment, and you are at the
moment occupying the place of the gentleman
from Poland. But if you will take my place, I
will gladly stand in the corridor."

But the gentleman from Poland wanted to
close the subject. "It is finished," he said im-
patiently, "make an end of it!"

I made an end of it, and shortly afterward
Aspasia and I went in to dinner.

We had dinner with the gentlemen from
Hungary and Bohemia. We were somewhat
satirical on the subject of the blond lady in the
cravenette coat. I amused the Hungarian gentleman by calling her *Elene von Troja*, likening
her to the beautiful woman who launched a
thousand ships and burnt the topless towers of

Ilium. But the Bohemian gentleman hushed us up. He wanted to avoid all international complications. When we returned to our compartment, the blond lady had departed. *"Die schöne Dame ist fortgegangen!"* exclaimed the Hungarian gentleman.

The man with the beard had not yet returned, and we were forced to the conclusion that he had been gone all the while. He had left the train before the arrival of the blond lady.

After all, she had been right; there was a vacant place all along. And she naturally wanted a seat. But just the same, I did not like the way she referred to my Italian: "I do not understand German; I don't care for that language!"

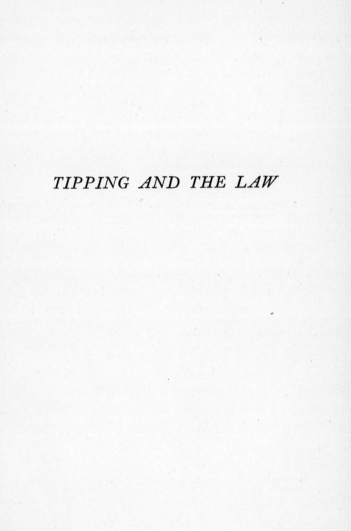

TIPPING AND THE LAW

V

TIPPING AND THE LAW

O UR man beguiled the tedium of the return from Tivoli with a lecture on politics. I may as well say at once that he was a sort of radical, though he always referred to himself as a Democrat. He thought that what they needed in Italy now was a little more freedom. The dictatorship was justified in the beginning, when the selfish sabotage of the railway men had threatened to run the country on the rocks. Much good had come to the country from the leadership of the man in the saddle. But the man in the saddle did not sufficiently understand the psychology of the men on foot. His intentions were no doubt good. But he wanted to reform the people against their will.

He was persuaded, the great leader, that all the country needed was to get back to work. (That certainly had a familiar ring to American ears. How many a banker, how many a man of state had brought us that cheerful message!) Increased production, that was what Italy wanted, and increased production meant more work on the part of the laboring man, and the government was determined to spur the laboring man on to work—of all things!—by raising the taxes. Fantastic it certainly sounds, but that was unmistakably the explanation of our Italian guide, delivered in good Dago English of Jersey City. The taxes at the gates of cities had been raised by some perfectly incredible percentage, and all with the purpose of goading the people on to work. Our guide was of the opinion that it was just as likely to goad them on to idleness and mischief. In his opinion there is a level of indigence below which a people cannot fall without losing its stamina. In his opinion the government was not reckoning with human nature.

Now politics is a subject which I do not profess to understand. Still less do I profess to understand political economy, that favorite plaything of nations and races, from which they get so many cuts and bruises, and which seems to have been the death of more than one of them. But human nature is a subject, however dark, on which one cannot help making his observations. And I had already observed for myself an instance in which the fascist government had notably failed in a laudable effort to regulate human nature. The institution of tipping has been officially abolished in Italy.

Joyous news to all travelers, who have so long trembled before this bugbear of the *pourboire*, this everlasting ordeal from which they are so desirous of coming off with honor! Whoever has left an English hotel without many an anxious conference with his wife, his conscience, and his pocketbook? How he has had to plan to find the chambermaid or the boots at the right moment, to get enough money in change to go round, to get it in small enough change so that he will not be compelled to give a sovereign where half a crown will do, and to find the right words with which to grace this graceless transaction! How long he has balanced between the prescriptive ten per cent and the generous twenty! He does not wish to be unjust to the men and women who are so largely dependent on him for the support of their industrious lives. He does not, on the other hand, wish to overdo his giving. In this he is moved by many strong reasons: what he owes to other travelers, what he owes to his own budget, and above all, his sovereign obligation, in a world of bargaining, not to be got the better of. With what a sigh of relief he sinks into his carriage and bids farewell to the scene of his worries, only to sit up a moment later in the stress of deciding what he should give to the driver!

In France the matter is simpler, so far as hotels are concerned, at any rate the modest hotels with which I have had dealings. The French are notoriously more logical and less individualistic than the English, and they don't expect you to deal individually with the *concierge*, the waiter, the head waiter, the boots, and the chambermaid. Instead of all this fuss, you go through a pleasant little ritual with the proprietor or proprietress. She hands you with a smile the long, stamped paper containing the items of your consumption. You glance through it, just for the form of the thing, for you have learned that you are not going to be cheated, though you may come on items that you had forgotten. Madame asks sweetly if it is *juste*, and you say, "Certainly." You take out your pocketbook and draw forth certain bills; Madame looks a bit wistful; and then you give a little start, and say, "*Tenez, Madame*, there is nothing here for service; will you be good enough to include the proper sum and distribute it for me?" "With pleasure, Monsieur," replies Madame, and without further remark adds the ten per cent, and hands you back the bill receipted.

That way everyone is satisfied. The proprietor is insured against a discontented personnel. The servant knows to a practical certainty that he will get his fee, and how much he will get. There is nothing arbitrary about the allotment, as there might so well be if it were left to an ignorant stranger. Madame knows well, and everyone on the staff knows well, the place of each in their little hierarchy, and what proportion he is entitled to receive.

There is still a pleasant margin of chance. Special services may receive special acknowledgment. Some particularly mean or thoughtless person may go off without leaving anything for gratuity. Someone on a honeymoon, or some vain, good-natured newly-rich may scatter largess on every hand. But in the main the business proceeds with the regularity of any other business; with the regularity of law itself.

But there is nothing in the statutes. If there is a law in the matter, it is an unwritten one, with all the force of the general will. It is a moral sanction on which the French servant relies for his protection against the niggardliness of his temporary master. In Italy they have undertaken to regulate the matter by law. Everywhere one reads in unmistakable terms that the institution of the *mancia* has been absolutely abolished; that all servants and functionaries are absolutely prohibited from receiving fees.

And thereby a great strain has been put upon human nature as it is found in meridional climes. Many instincts are offended. First, there is the instinct of personal liberty, if sociology will permit me to use the word instinct in this loose way. Everyone has at once the desire to get around the law. This is a point that hardly needs laboring for Americans since the passage of a certain constitutional amendment. And then there is the love of giving. If your *mancia* is included in the bill as a certain legally prescribed percentage, there is no longer any merit in it; it ceases to be a free gift from your good nature. And the Italians are particularly fond of giving.

At first one might suppose that the large number of beggars which even today beset the way of the traveler in the South was the creation of the tourist himself, the inevitable response of poverty to the presence of comparative wealth. And that may be an element in the situation. But so far as I have observed, it is not the *Inglese*, the British and American traveler, who supports the Italian beggar. He has been too well trained in the principle of associated charities, of aid dispensed with discrimination by social experts. He has been warned against bogus cripples and pitiful madonnas who have repeatedly refused the offer of honorable employment. Every time that he gives to a beggar he feels that he has extended the reign of beggary. When he refuses to give, it leaves behind a sting at least as distressing as a mosquito bite. But he has given to the Red Cross, or the Friends' Relief Fund for Central Europe, a hundred times the sum of what he would give to all the beggars in Naples, and that must serve for lenitive to his discomfort at refusing charity.

The Italian, on the other hand, seems to have no scruples at dispensing coppers to beggars. He is sorry for the poor devils and wants to help them. Moreover, it is an ancient and honorable Christian custom, which cannot do him aught but good in his religious capacity. It certainly gains him a thousand prayers for his happiness and salvation. It is likewise the part of the gentleman and *seigneur* to scatter largess. And it is equally an affirmation of the brotherly solidarity of poor mortals. The poor man gives as readily as the rich. I have known a fellow who earned his bread carrying bags to turn about and divide his drink-money with another man too old for aught but singing love ballads. He has known what it is himself to suffer want, and the day may come when he himself must solicit alms or go without bread. Perhaps the gift has in his feeling somewhat the character of an insurance against poverty.

You may wonder how I know so much about the state of mind of the Italian. It is simply that I have looked into my own mind. I think I must feel the same as the Italian, except that he, who lets himself give, feels it more often than I.

Whatever its components, it is a delicious feeling, and one much easier to entertain than to renounce.

And there is another passion of the southern heart, which I do not share to any great extent —but that is my loss—which is thwarted by the abolition of the *mancia*. That is the passion for taking a chance. This propensity is not, of course, confined to men of the South. Among the most constant patrons of Monte Carlo are certain great blond gentlemen brought up on the excitement of the Derby races, not to speak of the horde of respectable middle-aged English ladies who come to Monaco for the mild winter and stay to play the game. But it is evident that the love of chance has entered more into the fiber of the southern soul. A constant feature of their newspapers is the announcement of the lucky numbers in the lotteries. The children are as assiduous as their elders in the wooing of the fickle goddess. They will spend a morning throwing a copper or a single die, just to see how it may turn up. Any fine afternoon outside the Porta Romana at Florence, the Porta Asinaria at Rome, you will find an eager ring grouped about certain individuals with their faces chalked, who are engaged in raffling off sundry packages of sweet chocolate. It is a swarm of schoolboys and girls who love to take their chance of winning a handful of *regali* at hardly less than the price at the store, or, more likely, losing the coin which they put upon the hazard.

The love of uncertainty is as widespread as the love of security, and there are plenty of people who would rather not know just how much they can count on in the way of income. They would rather get little or nothing three times out of four, on the chance of getting the fourth time quite a good deal. The waiter who knows just what he is going to make off his dinner party has nothing further to occupy his mind and keep him in good humor, once the order has been given and the percentage computed; whereas if he is uncertain whether he will get fifty centimes, two francs, or five francs, he has wherewith to sweeten his meditations for the whole period of the repast.

The situation must have been a very bad one in Italy to have driven the government to such drastic measures, to such a defiance of many of

the strongest sentiments of the race. And so far
as concerns hotels and pensions, I fancy the results have been fairly satisfactory. Here and
there, to be sure, there are signs of weakening.
Tips are certainly offered at times by nervous
guests, and calmly accepted with a *troppo gentile,
signore!* There is always the matter of "special
services," and always much uncertainty as to
what constitutes a special service. I have lis-
tened to an argument between two American
ladies, one of whom was moved by her heart and
the other by her conscience. Heart was much at-
tached to the chambermaid, and had given her a
fee for what she called a special service. Conscience protested in the name of law and the
general interest. What special service, she demanded, had been rendered? Heart was somewhat put to it to make out a case. "Well," said
Heart, "she brought in my water-pitcher!" And
Conscience wanted to know what was the ordinary service of a chambermaid if bringing in the
water-pitcher was to be considered special.

And then certain other means are found of
making something "on the side." At a hotel
which caters to English tastes, you are engagingly

urged to take with your breakfast some honey
of Sorrento; and on yielding to this gentle solici-
tation you learn that the honey of Sorrento is
provided by the waiter himself, and that the
amount charged goes not into the bill, but into
the pocket of the man who brings your breakfast.
You send your suit out to be pressed; it is the
boots whom you pay. And if twenty-five lire
seems a high charge for the service, you realize
that the excess really stands as the perquisite of
the boots, and that this is his little way of getting
around the law.

But on the whole they find it to their advantage in the hotels to obey the law in regard to
the *mancia*. And life is thereby so much better
worth living in Italy. It is when you come to restaurants and cafés that you find the law actually
breaking down. There, too, the *mancia* is supposed to be included in the bill; and indeed, if
you receive a bill, you find the item, the ten per
cent, or whatever percentage it is that prevails
in that café, plainly added to the amount for
coffee and cakes. And generally you can take
your change and get away and no one will make
any fuss. Or, if there is no written account, but

you are informed orally of the amount of your indebtedness, you may inquire whether the service is included, and generally the waiter will reply, as by law required, "Certainly, sir, service is included." You hear them asking this question all over Italy, in German, English, French, Italian, and Slovak. And you can take the waiter at his word. But many circumstances tend to undermine your feeling of satisfaction in this state of things. The next time you go to the same café you are likely to be charged considerably more for the same refreshments. Or, if you inquire again whether the *mancia* is included, the waiter will answer "Certainly," and then he is likely to discover that he has not charged you sufficiently for the cakes consumed; that particular variety of *biscotti* is more expensive, being imported from England.

If your command of the language is sufficient, you may protest. You ask to see the card, or you call for the head waiter, and you may succeed in rectifying your account. But you will never go again to that café, which may be the most convenient one in the city. And in any case it is not your ambition to go about the world quarreling over *mancias*. You have spoiled your "five o'clock." You have lost your sense of being a man of the world, who leaves behind him a smiling restaurant, and carries away a whole-souled *a rivederla, signore*. You might just as well go without sugar in your coffee.

And then you begin to notice that Italians at cafés tip the waiter as a matter of course. You take your coffee standing at a bar, and the barman calls across the amount to the cashier in the most open manner: "Coffee, one lira; twenty centesimi, mancia!" You don't think a foreign traveler can be less generous than a native, or more scrupulous about the law. And you inquire of the *concierge* at your hotel whether you should not tip the waiters in cafés. The *concierge* replies gravely: "The tip is included in the bill." "Yes, I know," you reply, "but I often see people . . . ." "Well, one usually does give fifty centimes or a lira." (And you begin to have an uncomfortable feeling as to the correctness of your procedure as affects *concierges*.)

And the net result of it all is that, in a country where tipping is abolished, you go about paying double tips, and even triple ones, if you are justi-

fied in your suspicion that the foreigner is paying
ten per cent more than the native to begin with.
And it has even come about that in certain teashops chiefly frequented by foreigners the guest
is warned that the *mancia* is not included in the
bill, and, by inference, that he is expected to
provide that extra. On one side of the Via Tor-
nabuoni in Florence you are informed in the international language with which Italians address
English-speaking people: *Le pourboire est compris*, and on the other side: *Le pourboire n'est pas
compris*. And you choose the latter alternative
as being the cheaper! Certainly in these places
the abolition of the *mancia* has plunged the
whole subject into the most farcical confusion
and greatly added to the expense of the traveler
who does not wish to pass for a "tightwad."

Equally confusing is the situation as regards
services that are supposed to be governed by a
tariff, like that of porters and cab-drivers. The
matter is complicated by the fact that with these
men you have no English-speaking proprietor to
protect you, and that they are not provided, like
so many waiters in cafés, with a sufficient knowledge of English or French to do business with you

on a basis of something like mutual understanding. But the primary fact here is that the tariff is not high enough to bring these men a decent living. Seven cents is not enough to pay a man for steering you from the Naples-Rome train to the Rome-Florence train, carrying your three heavy bags, finding you window seats in a non-smoker compartment, and bidding you God-speed. How many trains can a man meet a day, and how many clients can he pick up in the fierce rivalry of porters, and what is the price of maca-roni, that the government allows him fifty cen-times a bag from train to train? Is it any wonder that when you offer him fourteen cents—knowing it to be twice the tariff—he tells you that the tariff allows him twenty-five, and that when you cite to him the exact terms of the tariff, he falls back on the fact that your bags are very heavy? It is against your principles to pay three times the tariff in a world where charity begins at home. And if you are eventually brought to giving a five-lira note to all porters without any regard for the tariff, it is no doubt simply out of your love for peace. But you might have come to it sooner from considering that the stout men who carry your bags must be fed, or there will be no more stout men to carry your bags. In any case, you have arrived, in a country where tips are abolished, at giving a tip of two hundred and fifty per cent of the nominal value of the original service.

As for cab-drivers—but that is another story, much too long for telling here. Only note that, in bargaining with these gentry, underpaid and rapacious, you must settle well in advance not merely the price of the service, but also that of the tip: so much for the drive, so much for the *mancia!* And the guardians of museums—another long story. I cannot undertake to follow this theme through all its fantastic changes to its absurd conclusion. Strong in humanity is the force of negative suggestion. The government of Signor Mussolini has forbidden by law the giving and taking of fees. And one has the impression that at the present time fees are accepted in Italy by anyone to whom they are offered, and solicited by everyone to whom they are not offered. It will even happen to the traveler—as it happened to me—to be approached by a smiling ruffian, a man whom I had never seen before, and one who had certainly never done me any service, with the simple statement: "I have need of a *mancia* from you." This statement was made in Italian, a language not well known to me, but I understood it perfectly, and it seemed as natural as if he had said: "Can you tell me the time of day?"

DOORKEEPERS

VI

DOORKEEPERS

> I had rather be a doorkeeper in the house
> of the Lord. . . . .

DMIRABLE is the provision of European churches for the support of the gentry necessary to the care of the premises. It is, naturally, impossible to charge admission to a church. But there is hardly a church worth visiting in any European country which hasn't some cloister, some chapel or sacristy, which enshrines the very holy of holies for the pilgrim of art or of piety. To attain unto this sanctum he must have recourse to the man with the key. And he will naturally leave in the palm of the doorkeeper some token of gratitude for the trouble to which the latter has gone in turning the key. Where there is no door to open, it is a guardian without imagination who cannot find some other means of earning his legitimate fee. In the Cathedral of Saint Andreas at Amalfi he will conduct you to the crypt, and after instructing you duly as to its age and manner of decoration, he will lead you to the tomb of Saint Andreas himself, and indicating the lamp burning before the sacred relic, he will suggest that five lire will be the natural contribution of your piety to the maintenance of this flame to perpetuity.

If there is any piety in you, or any love of historical beauty, you will never begrudge this little tax for the support of religion and art. You will wish, indeed, that there were more often a box in which you might deposit your contribution for the restoration or keeping up of the monument. Unfortunately, there is something about the way those five lire go into the pocket of the sacristan that suggests that Saint Andreas himself will never profit by your generosity. And yet, they have been designated as for the dead saint, and when you reach the door of the church you are uncertain whether you ought not to make some acknowledgment of his kindness to the living sacristan, whose flame requires more feeding than the other. And so a fifty-centesimi piece goes to join the five lire in the pocket of the sacristan. And then you learn that there is a highly interesting cloister to be entered by a special doorway, with a special guardian appropriated to it. And when you have visited this and made proper acknowledgment to its doorkeeper, you are confronted with five old women who have nothing to show you, to be sure, but whose flames likewise need sustaining by your generosity. And indeed it is seemingly thus that certain ancient towns are maintained with their whole populations.

There are some institutions which have failed to organize so well the means of supporting their caretakers. If I overdid my generosity at the shrine of Saint Andreas, I am afraid I underdid it at the shrine of the poet Keats. Lovers of English poetry never fail to visit at Rome the house in the Piazza di Spagna where John Keats spent his last miserable days under the devoted care of his friend Joseph Severn, and where now is maintained a collection of memorials of Keats, of Shelley, Byron, Hunt, Trelawny, and others associated with them. You are admitted to these rooms by a handsome and urbane young Italian, who finds a place for your dripping umbrella, and leaves the clerical work in which he is engaged to accompany you with silent discretion while you take down books from the shelves or examine MS letters in the cases. He answers your questions courteously in halting English, restores your umbrella, and lets you out. And when you have started down the stairs you begin to wonder how this admirable work is maintained, and whether it would not be more gracious to offer your mite to such a cause. That is what I wondered, at least, and I made my way back to the door, punched the bell a second time, and inquired of the guardian whether I might not make a slight offering for the maintenance of the house. "An offering," he replied, with a little brightening of his eyes, "an offering—oh yes, for the maintenance of the house. I must set down your name in the book." And he did produce a little account-book, and entered my five lire along with my initials. By that time I was wondering whether it might be permissible to offer a slight contribution to his personal maintenance. What if his clerical work which I had remarked were really the labor of a scholar—of a poet? What if his decent dress were really the mask of poverty? What if his salary from the institution consisted in such personal fees as he might receive from visitors? He seemed to have hesitated slightly at my suggestion of an offering. Was it perhaps that he was uncertain whether the offering were for the Keats memorial or for himself? Questions hitherto unanswered. For I had not the courage to offer a *pourboire* to so gentlemanly a guardian.

As for museums, it is well known that in Italy the government has officially condemned the giving of fees, and everywhere the eye is delighted with signs stating in the most uncompromising terms that the personnel is forbidden to accept them. But it is equally well known that this is a law more honour'd in the breach than the observance. In the great National Museum in Naples—one of the most important in the world for historical and artistic interest—it is impossible to obtain a catalogue of the collection. And I cannot imagine any reason for this state of things except the desire to deliver over the visitor to the tender mercies of the guardians of the museum. It is, at any rate, impossible to go through the rooms without receiving the instruction and guidance of half a dozen

uniformed men who are anxious to pick up a
few pennies. And if one has the force of character to reject their proffered assistance with
the necessary brutality, one's pleasure in the
works of art is largely impaired by the consciousness of this swarm of insects hovering about in
the neighborhood, always ready to swoop down
upon one in an unguarded moment.

And that is not the only inconvenience en-
tailed by this system of blind leading the blind.
Without the guidance of the printed word one
may easily get into places unforeseen, under circumstances not a little embarrassing. Thus it
was with Aspasia and me when we started to
visit the rooms in the Naples Museum devoted
to the spoils of Pompeii. At the first door
that we entered we were approached by an
official urgently inviting us to visit certain special rooms mysteriously indicated by his tone of
voice as being of particularly high interest to
the connoisseur. To this suggestion we readily
yielded, it being an article of our philosophy not
to swim too hard against the stream. This is,
in general, an excellent principle for the traveler
to follow. All sight-seeing is an adventure, and

it is naturally the uncharted regions of any continent that yield the most interesting discoveries.
In this case our guide turned us over to another
uniformed official at the door of the interesting
rooms. Our curiosity was heightened by the
somewhat anxious inquiry of the doorkeeper if
Aspasia were accompanying me. It was evident
that not everyone was to be admitted to these
precincts. I reassured him with a coin in the
palm.

And then the plot was thickened by the
appearance out of the wings, as it were, of an
estimable maiden lady from our pension, a
Dutch woman of a certain age, who had shown
us much friendliness on our first arrival and to
whom we owed every deference. This lady was
attracted by the general air which we must
have had of being on the track of something
particularly good, and her manner indicated a
disposition to make one of our party. It was all
the matter of a moment, and whatever communication passed between us must have been
in the form of nods and murmurs rather than
in that of articulate words of explanation, since
in any case we were not in a position to explain

anything except that we were pleased to encounter so agreeable a person. Another coin in the hand of the keeper, and we were all inside the first of the rooms in question.

There was quite a number of other guests, but no women whatever except those of my own party. And that is a peculiar circumstance in any museum to which European travelers are admitted. One glance at the walls showed me at once how the land lay. These were, indeed, Pompeian memorials of the highest interest—the Bouchers and Fragonards of that civilization that so much suggests by its elegance and luxury the age before the Revolution—Bouchers and Fragonards of buried Pompeii, but without that decorous grace and restraint which is always manifested by even the most provocative of the French painters of gallantry. I could not see what was contained in the second room, where were gathered the larger number of visitors, but I vaguely remembered what had been told me, by some archaeological friend, of the Rabelaisian humor of the ancients in their treatment of the mysteries of generation. I was not afraid for Aspasia, knowing how well her mind was disciplined by the critical spirit of university studies. Of the temper and training of our companion I knew little, or how much of philosophy and the historical spirit she might bring to this encounter. I immediately suggested to her that we had blundered into a roomful of improper pictures. She showed no signs of alarm, but went on placidly examining the exhibits. She did not linger over them, however, and soon she had passed into the second room. And then, all of a sudden, we saw her turn sharply about, and without a glance to right or left she sped straight past us, straight past the doorkeeper, and out of the fatal door.

Another of our adventures turned out more happily, another occasion when we yielded to the suggestion of the moment and saw sights not provided for in our itinerary. And this time we were made acquainted with still another type of doorkeeper, one unlicensed by any official position to ply his trade. Every ancient institution has sundry vagrant unauthorized forms of life rooting in its crevices, subtle and impudent parasites that would dishonor the edifice if it were not so noble, but which as it is do but color

and enliven the august masonry. No exception
to the rule is that most ancient and august of
Roman institutions, the Vatican. And of this
we were made aware by the accident of trying
to visit the Vatican museums on a day when
they were closed. We had been courteously informed by the Swiss guard that the Vatican was
closed on account of the fête: the Pope was
that day celebrating in the Sistine Chapel the
second anniversary of his coronation. But as we
turned away in disappointment at a morning
lost, we were hailed in friendly fashion by a
little man in a blue necktie who wanted to know
if we shouldn't like to see the Holy Father as he
returned to his apartments from the service of
the mass. This appealed to us as an excellent
way of recouping our loss, and our ardor was
only slightly dampened by learning of the large
number of lire which the little man would expect for his services in introducing us into the
palace.

It had never occurred to us to arrange for an
audience with the Pope after the fashion of so
many English and American travelers who cannot claim that privilege on the grounds of reli-

gion or business of state. We were eager sight-seers; but we had too much respect for his religion and office to wish to make him an object of vulgar curiosity. But now that an occasion had presented itself, so unsought, so providentially, one might say, we realized that (religion apart) there was no sight in Christendom better worth seeing than the supreme pontiff of the Catholic church—no personage or institution that has more to say to the philosophic mind. It is he who sums up in his office and person more than anything else the enduring tradition of ancient Rome.

Amid the undistinguished squalor and the still more undistinguished elegance of twentieth-century Rome, it is everywhere the substantial presence of the ancient city, even in its fragments, that makes itself felt with a certain awful and mysterious insistence. Even the street cars are given dignity by the great initials which they carry of the senate and people of Rome, S.P.Q.R. Over the mud and market wagons of the Via dei Conti rise a few elegant capitals and a section of the impressive walls of the Forum of Augustus. It is the column of Marcus Aurelius that gives quality to the merchandising galleries of the Piazza della Colonna.

And in modern Rome it is the churches and the church that have incorporated the most of ancient Rome. It is not merely that they have adapted the Pantheon to Christian worship and applied the bronze of its portico to beautify Saint Peter's; that everywhere one finds the columns of Roman temples built into the walls of churches that have taken their place. They have incorporated and adapted not merely the bodily tabernacle, but the religious spirit of the ancient *cultus*, its festivals, and many of the leading motives of its worship. And, in the bishop of Rome, they have taken over the very office of the high priest of the ancient state. No one who has scanned the brazen ode of Horace can fail to thrill to the very sound of the words *Pontifex Maximus*. Horace boasted that his songs would be sung so long as the high priest should continue to mount with the vestal virgin the steps of the Capitol:

dum capitolium
Scandet cum tacita virgine pontifex.

And if Horace will but accept the present assumption of the term, he may rest confident of an extended immortality, perhaps as great as that he anticipated. Surely he knew enough of history to realize the mutability of human affairs; he may even have foreseen the displacing of the Roman gods, and the day when Apollo and Mercury and Venus should be relegated to the museums of the Vatican as beautiful and harmless specimens of misguided religious zeal!

And so we lent ourselves willingly to the plans of the little man who wanted to smuggle us into the palace of the Vatican. For he had, of course, no authority to sell us those blue tickets of admission. As he said himself, he had a friend somewhere within the gates, with whom no doubt he would have to divide the proceeds of his little graft. And we were warned, in case of questions asked, to reply that the tickets had been given us at our hotel. We didn't like that very well, and we were relieved in the end not to have to secure a sight of the Holy Father at the cost of a lie. But there were other conditions almost as hard to accept. It seemed that Aspasia's hat, though perfectly correct according

to worldly standards, would not seem decorous
in the sacred presence. And so there would be a
little item of lire to be expended at the Pellegrino Cattolico for a decent black scarf to be
worn in its place. Aspasia was not particularly
averse to that, since pretty ladies always look
more fetching in a black lace scarf. But then
it appeared that the proper thing to do was to
secure a rosary, likewise at the Pellegrino Cattolico, which would share in the papal blessing,
and remain always a memento of the occasion,
concentrating, as it were, in its material form
the spiritual essence of the ceremony.

Now Aspasia didn't like at all proceedings
which had so much the air of a masquerade.
Moreover, she rightly suspected that the rosa-
ries to be had at the Pellegrino were showy,
rather than beautiful or artistic. She confessed
to the little man that she was not a Catholic, but
he replied that, while that was a pity, it didn't
really make any difference in the spirit of the
thing, and he remained quite firm in his per-
suasion that she should have a rosary, and one
of the type in which they dealt at the Pellegrino
Cattolico. So these things were secured, As-

pasia's hat was left in the care of the sales-woman of the Pellegrino, the little man received his item of lire, and we started up through the great colonnade and entered the door of the palace.

By this time we were rather ashamed of the whole business, and felt that we cut but a sorry figure as we mounted the steps of the royal stairway and entered the Sala Regia. (I was conscious myself of my rather gay overcoat from the Galeries Lafayette, my summer gray trous-ers, and my cane of malacca.) But we had laid out by now quite a little sum of lire; no one seemed to notice what sort of figure we cut; and we felt bound to go through with the thing.

And now we were absorbed in the spectacle itself. The Sala Regia was a hall worthy of these great doings, and eloquent of the secular power of the popes, painted as it is with subjects like the Battle of Lepanto and the submission of the Emperor Henry IV at Canossa. Equally satis-fying were the traditional uniforms of the papal officials—stupendous guards in hats that added several feet to their height, and civil officers in knee breeches and dress coats of red velvet and

satin. Knots of monks were politely discussing
in French matters of interest to them, and soli-
tary priests were pacing the floor reading their
prayers. At the end of the hall nearest the chapel was a dense group of those most anxious to
have a good view of the procession, mostly
ladies with faces framed in black lace scarves,
and eager young theological students, for whom
this occasion would furnish matter of talk for a
lifetime.

The people of most importance were naturally in the chapel assisting at the service. It was
later that we had an opportunity of observing
as they left the hall the men and women of
secular quality who enjoyed this privilege, and
so of receiving an ocular impression of that curious, or at least for us mysterious, little world of
papal society. Very fine they were to the eye—
men magnificent in court dress and covered with
glittering orders, and grand ladies, all of them
looking Spanish princesses in their lace mantillas,
and one of them we knew must be a queen, since
we were told that no less a personage was actually present at this service. There were elderly
ladies whose proud gray faces were expressive of

serene authority, from whom an invitation is a command, and whose invitations are no doubt as assiduously sought as any in Mayfair or the Faubourg Saint-Germain. There were beautiful young women greeting their friends among the officers with smiles that were equally powers in the social world. It was pleasant to find such flowers blooming in these grave precincts. Of the men, some were tall, handsome fellows perfect in the management of the single eyeglass. Some were bald and unimposing, and the magnificence of their decoration did but set off their insignificance. And yet who knows? It is perhaps this most ridiculous fussy little man, in the prestige of his office or character, who wields the greatest power, and whose favor is most courted by high and low. It was useless to speculate on the constitution of this little state, what motives govern conduct there, what goals are sought, what wheels within wheels control its movements; to imagine by what services or by what native merit one obtained entrance and standing in this society. We had not the key to this door. And we could only remind ourselves that the state of "society" is natural to humanity in all conditions; that all forces upon earth operate through social instruments; and that wherever there is an institution dispensing prestige, be it but a university or a labor union, there will be a throng of people eager to fill their pitchers at the fountain of honor.

But all this was after the return of the Pope from the Sistine Chapel—a rite accomplished with simple and majestic state. There was first the passage of cardinals and high ecclesiastics. Of these we could see little over the heads of the throng, only now and then the splendor of scarlet and ermine, with a clerical profile massively molded or delicately chiseled. But the Holy Father was lifted high in his pontifical chair, so that none might fail to see his face and his gesture of benediction. He made, certainly, an impressive figure in his long white gown magnificently embroidered with gold, and his gold-embroidered triple crown. It was the fine, white, spectacled face of Pius XI; features strong, shrewd, and benevolent, the face of a churchman and a statesman. Behind him moved, on either side, two great ceremonial fans of ostrich plumes, of oriental splendor. But pomp and personality were sunk in the sense of the sacred office. And while the *evvivas* of the theological students accompanied his slow progress across the end of the hall, he continued to move back and forward his white hand with two extended fingers in the traditional, hieratic, and gravely dramatic gesture. We had by now forgotten the humiliating shifts by which we had gained admission, and we realized only that we were in the presence of that one of earthly potentates who retains the most of ancient dignity and significance, the sole remaining depository of the prestige of the Roman Empire.

As for the man in the blue necktie, we saw him the next day in the museum of the Vatican. He was guiding a tourist through the apartments of the Borgia. We hailed him as an old friend. And he did not deny our acquaintance. But he made no allusion at all to the service in the Sistine Chapel, and the blue tickets of admission.

THE BEGGAR IN THE FORUM

ASPASIA was happy because she had found a tuft of wild iris blooming among the rubble of the Forum. It was near the Fountain of Juturna, the ancient goddess of waters, and not far from the temple of Vesta, goddess of the sacred fire. We were at the very hearth of the ancient worship, the center of Roman theology, now to be traced by the learned eye in a few fragments of altar, frieze, and statue. Above us on their high base rose three graceful columns in marble, all that remains of the temple of Castor and Pollux, and we read that this temple had been built to commemorate the miraculous appearance of the twin gods after the battle of Lake Regillus; they had ridden hither to announce the victory of the Romans, and they paused to water their steeds at the spring of Juturna. The ancient gods were all gone, together with the heroes who fostered their worship, and the comely worship of fire and water. But the blooming iris were like an oracle, some hopeful word of the goddess Nature herself, assurance of her divine persistence. At least they were a promise of spring, which we had sought in vain through months of chill and rain.

And so we climbed in cheerful mood to the foot of the pillars, where we might have a view of the whole Forum, and lay out intelligently our plan of antiquarian research. We looked forward to a morning of peaceful browsing among ruins. But scarcely had we reached our post of vantage and settled down to a bit of preliminary basking in the sun when we became aware of someone approaching as if to address us. It was a pimply-faced young man with his coat collar turned up, who inquired in French for the time of day. I readily informed him that it was quarter to eleven, glad to be relieved so easily of the threatened intrusion on our privacy. But it was not to be so easy as that. For now the young man wanted to know, half in French, half in Italian, whether we shouldn't like to take him for guide through the monuments of the Forum.

Our negative was automatic. It is our first instinct always to say no to the offer of guidance. The would-be guide is a nuisance in the same category with the peddler and the life-insurance agent; he presents a problem to a mind unprepared to cope with it. And that is reason enough to refuse his services, if he were not, into the bargain, as pushing and pertinacious as the peddler and the life-insurance agent. He obliges one not merely to refuse, but to refuse curtly, scornfully, if one is to get rid of him; and God knows that the necessity of thus doing violence to the mildness of our nature does but add to our irritation and sharpen the edge of our denial. And then a guide costs money, and that is something not provided for in our budget. And if we are reconciled to spending something on a guide, there remains the question of how much. We must either begin by making a bargain, and so enter upon our sight-seeing with ruffled spirits; or we must suffer the still greater torment of speculating throughout the expedition on the sum which will satisfy him at the end, and save us from the final ignominy of a mercenary dispute. These guides, moreover, are so often mendacious and ill informed, and they speak such an unintelligible jargon, and they hurry one so ruthlessly past sights that deserve the most leisurely consideration. But above all, and first of all, they are an intrusion on one's privacy. With a guide on your hands you can neither study, nor meditate, nor make love—and what else should be the objects of a visit to the Forum?

And so Aspasia and I came out with our "No!" as simultaneously as the first and second gentlemen in a Shakespeare play; we preferred not to have a guide. But the pimply young man is not so readily put off. And he proceeds to mention dinner as something desirable to which he will be helped by our concurrence in his plans. That puts a new face upon things. Who mentions dinner appears in the light of a beggar, and beggars are more simply disposed of. I determine to offer him money as a means of getting him off our hands. But first my conscience dictates a question or two as to his condition, and the causes of his beggarly state. His clothes are not those of a beggar, nor of a guide, for that matter. His upturned coat collar indicates a desire to disguise a want of shirt collar which would pass for matter of course with one whose home was in the streets. And I am not surprised to learn that he has been employed in a lawyer's office, but that the times are hard, and that the lawyer has been obliged to dispense with his services.

It is a plausible case. And while the pimply face and irresolute mouth of our young man make it clear that he is no thrifty young Stinnes out of luck, I am not one to hold against a man an irresolute mouth. An irresolute mouth is but one misfortune the more. I am reminded of an institution at Paris which impressed me with its humaneness of spirit. There is not far from the great municipal hospital of the Rive Gauche a pretty cottage in soft tan stucco with large green-shuttered windows, and a sign beside the door indicates that it is a free home for nursing mothers, "with no questions asked." That is surely the spirit in which, in this world, such a phenomenon should be approached; with so much that is dark in the ways of destiny, the one certain thing is that mothers should be given a decent place to nurse their babies, irrespective of how they came by them.

It is not equally certain that one should give money to every young man with a weak mouth who wants to show you the monuments of ancient Rome because he is hungry. But my point is that any of us may come by a weak mouth through no fault of our own, and that hunger is a universal human experience. Moreover, it was most desirable that Aspasia and I should be left free to prosecute our antiquarian researches. And the upshot of it all was that I offered the young man the sum of one lira toward his dinner. He did not seem satisfied with that, and he began to murmur something which I took to be a statement as to the inadequacy of one lira in face of his need for dinner. But I cut him short with the remark that it was a beginning. *"C'est un commencement,"* says I, in my most reasonable tone, and the young man moved away in the manner of one who has met a defeat, sinking down still deeper into his upturned coat collar.

He was soon out of sight behind some mound of moldering brickwork, but he was not soon out of mind. It was long before we could summon spirit for our sight-seeing. We were, somehow, not well satisfied with the way we had come off from this encounter.

And why not? Was he not, in fact, a beggar? In the mind of the traveler these volunteer guides

are really but a species of beggars. They belong
to that numerous class of mendicants who lie in
wait for you at every turn in Latin countries, and
especially in Italy, under the guise of persons eager to do you a service. They would like to show
you the way to the Church of the Frari or to the
Piazza Sammarco! They would like to introduce
you to the night life of Paris, or to the Pompeian
dance at the Crystal Palace in Naples. Only the
unaccompanied man, to be sure, is liable to these
latter solicitations, and therein lies one great advantage of having a lady on your arm to exorcise
these devils. But the lady only makes things
worse at the church door, where they insist on
lifting the leather curtain for her to enter. In
the museums there is always someone whose sole
business in life is to relieve you of an umbrella
which is really no bother to you at all. In the
theater they are present in force and with due
empressement, to take your wraps, to show you
to your seat and push it down for you, to show
you the way to the toilet—smirking hags, grim
harpies, superannuated harlots, reaching out
their claws to rake in pennies! They know very
well the value of their service. They recognize

the foreigner at the length of the corridor, and they know how to work upon his innocence. They know how to set him right as to European customs. I have seen such an old woman in the top gallery of the Paris Opéra cast on the floor in scorn the few sous offered by an American, as a way of teaching what is due to a lady of her quality from a gentleman of his.

And then there is that class of beggarly persons who beset the highways wanting to sell you something. They have their special haunts. In Naples it is the vendors of articles in tortoise-shell for cigaret-smokers. They do a brisk business among American girls who put up at the great hotels, the Metropoles and Continentals, along the water front. At the Island of Capri it is the vendors of cheap coral that thrive. They hang about the excursion steamer that takes you to the mouth of the Blue Grotto. They first bring their wares to your attention as you wait for the little boat that takes you into the grotto. They besiege you on your way thither, and on your return, and they infallibly make a sale before the steamer starts back. In Paris and along the Riviera flourish the picturesque race of those who ply a business in oriental rugs. The rugs are obviously of cheap western manufacture, but the sellers are oriental enough (or is it African?) to make up for that, with their white teeth and their swarthy visages. And they certainly dress the part. At Menton I have seen as many as four of them at a time, with their white turbans and flowing white robes, perched on the seaside rocks like strange birds of prey, or displaying their bright tissues to the tourists taking their lunch on the hotel terrace.

I have never made out how the trade can support so many of these peddlers. It is hard to imagine to what taste they can appeal, and among the hundreds of them whom I have seen during a year in Europe I have known but one to make a sale. That was in the Café de la Paix in Paris one summer night, and it was the entertainment of the café for two hours to watch the bargaining and to lay bets as to which of the parties to this strange contest would have the best of it. The buyer was a New York Jew, who from the beginning professed to have no interest in the rugs, and who probably, as a matter of fact, had no use for them. But he could not resist the temptation to do a little bargaining. The most edifying feature of the affair was the inexhaustible patience and the heroic good nature of the salesman. For two hours he was on his feet on the busiest sidewalk in Paris. To us the case seemed a hopeless one, and we could imagine his inward rage as half-hour after half-hour of his precious time rolled away in the siege of one hard-hearted and indifferent customer. In point of fact, we could see his rage and discouragement darkening his face time and again, and time and again we saw him rallying his forces to show the grinning visage of imperturbable good nature that was his best stock in trade. In this case, certainly, virtue was rewarded. In the end he made his sale. I don't know what was the price paid for this wretched composition in red and blue cotton; but I feel sure that it was the smiling Algerian who got the best of the crafty nonchalant gentleman from New York. When Greek meets Greek. . . . .

In the cafés of Vienna these traveling salesmen have nothing so precious to offer as bogus Persian rugs, nothing, in fact, worth bargaining over. But they are sometimes pertinacious enough in their efforts to make a sale. I remember a man trying to sell court-plaster to a couple taking a sandwich after the play. He threatened to stick as tight as the article in which he dealt, and he was dismissed with what seemed to me an unnecessary degree of asperity. As for myself, I dismissed him too, but in a manner combining firmness with courtesy. And thereby Aspasia was moved to make not less than two of her shrewd observations. In the first place, she explained that this asperity was not necessarily the indication of a hard heart on the part of the person declining to buy. He was perhaps a man of limited means himself, who was obliged to take on this rough manner in order not to give in to his sympathetic inclination. And having thus defended the other man for his discourtesy in declining to buy, she began to reproach me for not buying. After all, she pointed out, here was a man trying to make an honest living. As it was, he could probably make more as a simple beggar. He should be encouraged in his laudable effort to remain independent and self-supporting.

I had to acknowledge it was a point well made. Since we had been in Vienna, the thing which

had impressed us as saddest in the state of the
Austrians was the prevalence of beggary. In Italy
we had no such feeling. From time immemo-
rial the Italians have made a fine art of begging. They have been brought up to it from in-
fancy. They have put into it all their gaiety, all
their pathos, all their dramatic art. And it is
with them an inveterate habit—that is, with that
debonair, hand-to-mouth, *dolce far niente* riffraff
that so strike the eye of the foreign sojourner.
Even when the Italian beggar is a cripple you suspect him of being a comedian, and there is something in his own manner that seems to acknowledge the impeachment. You think of the Cour
des Miracles in *Notre-Dame de Paris*, where all the
rogues of Paris congregated and made themselves
up for their begging or thieving raids upon the
bourgeois. Or you think of the film of *The Miracle
Man*, and the creature in the New York slums
who had such a happy faculty of twisting himself out of shape. There is a great deformed rascal
who sprawls on the pavement at the entrance to
the Vatican Museum in Rome, and solicits alms
of all who enter. He is not one of those surly
beggars who curse you for refusing to give. In

fact, I refused to give so many times, on my various visits to this museum, that there came to be a friendly understanding between us. We always greeted one another in the most smiling and amicable manner, like Roman augurs giving one another the wink. He seemed to say, in his jolly fashion: "I see you have my number, and I think I have yours in a general way, but I don't know what particular graft it is you work on a world that owes us a living. *Salute!*"

It is in the sunny South that they have most thoroughly organized that variety of volunteer service which undertakes to make you gay, to give a proper air of festivity to life in that land of pilgrimage *wo die Citronen blühn.* It starts at Nice, that still half-Italian city, with the ragged little girls whose mission in life it is to see that no lady goes without her bunch of violets or of golden mimosa. These zealous missioners will take no denial. They toss their flowers into the lady's bosom, and trot along beside you shaking their dark curls and smiling into your eyes—irrespective of sex—with a coquetry more convincing than the whine of the importunate widow. *Sourire est séduire.* Their cousins meet you in the steep street of Fiesole as you go up to take your view of Florence and the valley of the Arno, with their little fistfuls of faded daffodils; in the lemon-bordered lanes of Sorrento, with the first purple daisies. They toss their flowers into your carriage as you drive through Positano, high above the sea—and you have not the heart to dash in the dust these delicate tokens of supernal innocence and beauty.

The most approved way of making us merry in the land of music is with the power of melody. Who does not remember, in the old days, when the sunset was fading behind the Ponte Vecchio and the lights were coming out on the Piazzale Michelangelo, the lusty fellows who came to sing beneath the balcony, *O Sole Mio!* Or on summer nights in Siena the boys who go singing in the moonlight thoughtlessly—without money and without price—that lovely flower-like song of theirs, with its long, dying fall:

> Mi sono andato all' me-e-ssa
> Al campo sa-a-nto
> Sopra la tomba be-e-lla
> Del mio amo-o-o-o-re!

It was all one with the plashing of the Fonte
Branda, with the varied jangling of the campa-
nile bells, falling all day and all night like flower
petals through the enchanted air. But now—ah!
"What has befallen in the world of wonder?"
What is this thin melancholy music that one
hears in all the streets of Europe—the music box
on the corner in Vienna grinding out faded ball
tunes, unrecognizable Blue Danubes? This little
old man in the Boulevard Saint-Germain, with a
tin whistle which he plays with his nose? This
cracked voice beneath the balcony at Menton,
whining vaguely of love and beauty? This quaint
duet of the Ponte Santa Trinita, where Dante is
pictured as meeting Beatrice; the blind man playing the flute, and the cross-eyed man playing the
guitar? Even Italy has lost the art of street music; and never were there so many street musi-
cians as now, coming out whenever there is a bit
of sun, to make us merry with their faint symbols
and hieroglyphs of melody. Is it modernism that
has done this for Italy? Have they all turned to
motor cycles and modern improvements? Is it
the war that has left no lusty beggars, but only
ancient deaf men lost in retrospection?

They are mostly creatures incapable of rendering any other kind of service. And there is something cheerful about the bravery with which they turn to music rather than to simple beggary. It is indeed surprising how few there are who rely merely on their disabilities to make appeal to our charity. The *mutilés* are a class by themselves. They cannot fail to move your sympathy, whether you regard them in the light of victims or of a heroic voluntary sacrifice. In all countries they are much in evidence, even in France, where I am sure they need not go upon the streets to beg their bread. Our landlady informs us that the government makes provision for them; and she has little patience with men who make a public exhibition of their merits and their deformities. But it is clear that not all the world shares her feelings in this regard, or there would not be so many of these maimed soldiers making their silent ocular appeal in the subways, in the parks, on the bridges, throughout all Europe.

I have in mind a little scene in the Volksgarten in Vienna particularly eloquent of the complex sentiments involved in the act of charity. There was the good-natured young cripple in his wheel chair, who was taking advantage of a little watery sunlight to seek in the park for traces of delaying spring. There was the lady in black taking the air with her daughter—a little princess, fresh from the hands of her tiring-woman. It was the office of the child to present their alms to the poor cripple; and she went prettily through what must have been for her an adventure of some magnitude. She receives from her mother the note for a thousand kronen (of the value of a cent and a half), trots across to the wheel chair and presents it coyly, and then trots back safely to the protection of her mother's hand. The gift is graciously received, with a special smile for the Lilliputian princess. It was altogether an elaborate little ceremonial, and reminiscent of traditions as old as humanity. It was significant enough as a mere act of charity. But under the present circumstances it was complicated with all the emotions attending the Great War, and that in a country beaten and dismembered. I was reminded of the sensation in the Burgtheater on the recitation of certain lines from Goethe's *Iphigenie auf Tauris*. It is Pylades recounting to Iphigenia the outcome of the ten years' Trojan war, and naming the Grecian heroes who have left their bodies on the foreign shore.

I suppose our landlady is right about the *mutilés* who decline to accept the employment or the asylum provided by the government, preferring the tender mercies of the man in the street. But one office they do serve. They serve to remind us of the meaning of war. That is, they might serve to remind us of that, if humanity were apt to heed such object-lessons. But when we stop to consider that the case has always been the same, that history has never seen the time when the streets were not full of the victims of war. . . . .

The problem of the beggar is the most besetting anxiety of any conscientious traveler. At home he knows better where he stands. He knows what public agencies there are for the care of the needy. He has friends in the charitable organizations, and is informed as to the precise financial status of this blind man at the corner of Nicollet and Sixth, this legless man on the sidewalk by the bank. But abroad he is all in the dark, and he knows not whether the easy gift of a few sous will serve most to relieve distress or to encourage vice. He knows that begging is the habit of the lazy and the trade of the cheat. The church is a fertile breeding-place of beggars who take a rascally advantage of the Christian injunction to charity. They know that we come from a church with softened hearts, and sturdy boys approach you in the Piazza with a tin plate for your coins as if they were taking up a collection for the work of the gospel.

And there are so many other ways in which they come upon you opportunely. It may be after the theater, when you are in the expansive mood of one who has done his duty by his pleasures. It may be as you issue forth from an antiquarian shop, hugging under your arm some precious object "more than a hundred years old," which you have obtained at a figure so much below that originally named by the dealer. They are so easily put off, with a mere gesture of refusal, and they slink away like shadows into the dark places from which they emerged.

And there is always the chance that the beggar is actually a person in need, a person, it may be, on the brink of starvation. It is sometimes a

woman decently dressed, whom you cannot figure
in the rôle of professional beggar, and who has
not even the craft to carry an ailing baby in her
arms. She is not accustomed to begging, but she
has seen you come out of a shop, she has marked
the signs of your affluence, and instinctively
she has turned to you in her trouble. She cannot
speak your language, but she puts her fingers to
her mouth in sign of her need. You cannot speak
her language, and you do not know how to inform yourself in a scientific manner as to the
merits of the case. How can you turn your back
upon her? What right have you to deny her peti-
tion?

And suppose you could speak her language,
how likely is it that you would have the patience
or the wisdom to go really to the bottom of the
matter? What better off was I for my questioning of the young man in the Forum? Our landlady, who has not really a hard heart, has a
shrewd word to say on this subject. She says she
prefers to give without too much probing. She
has been taken in so often. She prefers to keep
her sentiment unspoiled: *garder ses sentiments*.

Ah, there is a deep word, *Madame la Patronne*,

and one that shows you a keen psychologist. To
keep our sentiment unspoiled! To maintain our
faith in human nature; first in ourselves, and
then in other men. It is our most constant passion, and one in which we are most constantly
disappointed. To keep an open heart—and not
to be taken in! No easy matter in a world so full
of misery and so full of fraud. If only we could
with a good conscience follow the precepts of
Christ, and treat all beggars simply as "God's
poor!" "And him that taketh away thy cloak
forbid not to take thy coat also!"

To keep our sentiment unspoiled! That was
where I came short with the young man in the
Forum. The trouble was that I treated him as a
beggar, when most likely he was nothing of the
sort. He was a man looking for honest employment, eager to reconcile his hunger with his self-
respect.

—But he took the money you gave him?

Well, yes, it was evident that he wanted his
dinner.

—And he was not content with what you
gave him?

Ah, there I am not so sure. He did make

some demur, but I cut him short in my impatience. Most likely it was not the amount of my gift to which he took exception, but the fact of my making him a gift. He did not want charity, he wanted employment. He wanted humane consideration. And I cut him short because I was in a hurry to visit the ruins of the Forum. And he sank his chin in his collar and turned away.

Oh, we are full of good sentiments, but we time them so poorly! Our best sentiments are most often only afterthoughts.

THE POET OF SORRENTO

VIII
THE POET OF SORRENTO

O N THE first sunny morning we sallied forth. We passed through the lanes among the villas and lemon groves. We ran the gauntlet of pretty boys offering violets and of engaging cabmen offering a lift. And we turned straight down to the landing-place. The little harbor was full of animation. The fishermen were patching up their boats, and some enchanting fragrance filled the air— something nostalgic and marine, which proved on investigation to be the smell of boiling pitch. And there in the little *piazza*, leaning against the mossy sea wall, we first really took in the matchless bay, spreading now with such amenity from the hanging gardens of Sorrento far across to the outlined hills of Ischia. In the center was a mild Vesuvius blowing meditative smoke-rings. It was gratifying to find the Mediterranean blue running so true to type; that blue that makes an underworld heaven of the grotto of Capri. Still

more to the point was the lucid green under the
cliffs, a green for Venuses to spring from in the
world of Botticelli.

And there, in a little embrasure of the sea
wall, sure enough, was the poet, without whom
what were heaven or Venus in a world of tourists and trippers?

He was not yet turned twenty, and but recently made acquainted with Virgil and Leo-
pardi. He wore the spectacles of a nearsighted
man, and he had on a new soft hat. We knew
him at once by his ferocious and furtive air. It
was not drawing-paper he held in his lap, and we
knew that no artist is so much afraid of being
observed. Artists one has seen in plenty, copy-
ing Andrea del Sartos in museums, or creating
Picassos at Saint Pol or Positano, and they always go on complacently enough beneath the
gaze of the most curious. It is only your poet
who is so jealous of his privacy, and who tucks
away so slyly the bits of paper on which he has
written words of fire, and pretends that he isn't
there.

We had no desire to break up an interview
with the Muse, and we moved on down to the

pier. There, for a while, we watched the boats pulling at their ropes. But we were much troubled with the solicitations of boatmen wanting to row us over to the Marion Crawford villa or in any way to put themselves at our disposal. And then Aspasia discovered a place where we could get coffee. Aspasia is a vigorous traveler, and always ready for some variety of refreshment. There is indeed, perhaps, no better way to hold communion with the sea than sitting in the sun on the veranda of a fisherman's café. And if there was a touch of prosiness in our proceeding, we felt entirely justified when, a few moments later, the poet himself appeared, took his place at a nearby table, and ordered something to eat.

He had doubtless breakfasted early, and felt the need of something to keep up his strength in the face of so much beauty. And what he ordered was no vulgar banquet of Lucullus, but the plain fare of the people—just the "macaroni of the family."

Macaroni is a word of simple magic to Italian ears. When the loafer on the dock has helped you into the boat and breathes the word "maca-

roni," he has in mind a twenty-centesimi piece
which may be applied to any of the simple needs
of life. When your driver is leaving you for your
luncheon at Amalfi and just stops to mention
macaroni, he means to remind you that he, too,
has to have something to eat, and that his purse
is lighter than yours. And the poet of Words-
worthian strain, when he asks for the family
macaroni, utters the word with reverence, as one
who loves the people with a deep love, and does
not deny his kinship with them.

Wine? No, said the poet, that would go to
his head. This was no jaded Horace seeking in-
spiration in Falernian! He would take a cup of
coffee and a bit of cheese.

He was not a bit less furtive or ferocious, but
he did venture, under the genial influence of the
family macaroni, to take out his bits of paper
and set down a few words, giving occasional
hasty glances over his shoulder at the sea. We
felt apologetic for our presence there, and dared
not speak above a whisper or give a sign of consciousness that he was there with the Muse beside him. And yet, who knows? Aspasia is not
herself so unlike a Muse. And in any case she is

a very pretty young woman. And while I am neither pretty nor young, this was a poet who shared with us the veranda and the bay. Lovers are surely as indispensable to the poet as the poet is to lovers. And indeed we were lovers in simple sooth. Who knows whether he may not have been as excited over us as we were over him? Who knows that we did not go to his young head like wine of Falerno?

When we came to go, I found I did not have in my pocket the two lire to pay for our coffee. If I had not put fifty centesimi in San Antonio's poor-box I should have had the sum required. The *padrona* was very good about it. She said that San Antonio's work was a good one, and that it didn't matter, and I said that we should certainly come back again and see that she was paid. And so we made our retreat, while the poet went on writing hasty words on his bits of paper.

And that is the last we ever saw of him. But we did learn a little more about him, to confirm us in our identification and finish his picture in our imaginations. We did go back to pay for our coffee, and I took the liberty of discussing our fellow-guest with the good woman of the place.

"That young man," I said, "was surely a poet?"

"A poet?" she replied. "Ah, the young man from Naples? Perhaps you are right. He was scribbling something on a sheet of paper. Only wait a moment."

She dived into the house, and returned with a crumpled sheet on which was a penciled scrawl in Italian. It was an unformed hand, and there were many false starts and erasures. But we managed to make out the broad lines of a grandiose and fervid figure of speech: "From the right hand and the left the land reaches out into the sea like the two arms of a man embracing. . . . ." Perhaps I was not so far wrong in suspecting that Aspasia and I counted for something in the passionate emotions of the poet.

But the landlady was inclined to note another aspect of the matter. "Poet! yes. As soon as you and the Signora were gone, he began to talk . . . . in such a manner! '*Ah, che bellezza! Com'è felice Lei!*' Ah, what beauty! How happy you to live forever in sight of so much beauty! Well, it is pretty today—and the first sunny day for weeks! All winter *cattivo tempo*—such horrid weather! And life so hard! What would you have? The fishermen are not rich, and I have all I can do to provide macaroni for my family. He did not require wine, your poet. That would go to his head. Coffee, yes. And for his dinner, the macaroni of the family!"

THE MODEL

IX
THE MODEL

S HE was a very good-looking woman. That was my first reflection, but I kept it to myself. I realized at once that it was irrelevant. No one in the place seemed to take any notice of her good looks, and least of all the woman herself. She sat patiently enough on her platform, lost in vacancy of mind, and in the resting-spells she marched around and stretched and warmed herself before the stove with as little consciousness of her personal appearance as if her sole covering had not been the rings in her ears. I could not help wondering why, with her good looks, she had not managed to assure her livelihood in some way more advantageous to herself. Heaven knows, beauty is no drug on the market. And there was no evidence that beauty was an asset to her in this school of painting. "Everybody prefers this room," said Lindgren, "because there is a better light. And the other model has a very white skin.

Léonie, on the other hand, has exceptionally warm flesh tints."

Outside the windows opposite Léonie was a little courtyard shut away from the street, with the lilacs beginning to come out and the sun a bit uncertainly touching the new leaves of the horse-chestnut. But no one seemed to take any notice of that, and I kept to myself whatever fancies occurred to me in that connection. I had not come there to give rein to my "literary" sense, but to inform myself on the process of painting pictures. There was nothing in the room but the stove, and the easels of the students, and the model's platform. She had behind her a bit of brown cloth and a bit of blue cloth, and she was sitting on a bit of white cloth.

And I found, as I went from easel to easel, that each of these young painters was making her more ugly than the last. Some had done her in pink, and some in orange; some in violet, and some in ashen gray. Little attention was given to the delicate lines of her figure, the effort being apparently to make her look like a wooden idol, greatly foreshortened in the upper parts of her body. Not much was left of her head, and the

only recognizable thing about that was the earrings. They had been working for a week, and
this morning the master was to make his comments. There was one man in particular who
seemed to me to be wasting his time. He did not
seem to have any sense of color, but he kept on
with a stubby brush, rubbing in a pinkish-brown
pigment over the whole surface of the picture in
a kind of consistency of dreariness. There was a
perverse logic about his procedure that suggested
obstinacy and cunning at work in the service of
dulness.

Finally the master came in, and everyone
stopped working, except the model. He is a highly considered painter, and one of the three or four
men in Paris whose word carries weight with students at the present moment. He was a work-
man-like little man in a blue shirt, such as you
might expect to find as foreman of a machine-
shop, with a little clay pipe to help him with
his gestures, but sparing of gesture, and going
straight to business. He began at one end of the
room, and worked his way to the other end, going down the rows of easels, with a word of critical suggestion for each canvas. The artists gath-

ered about him in a dense group to profit as a
body by his individual instructions; young men
and women from America and England, from
France and Sweden, anxiously watching for the
words which should open up for them the inner
secrets of the trade. And I, less professional, lis-
tened eagerly for some gospel of art, ready for the
flash of insight with which he might illumine the
aesthetic problem in general. And this is the gist
of what he said, standing before one easel after
another, waving his clay pipe delicately here and
there over the surface of a canvas, and with an
occasional glance at the model to verify some
fact of color and light:

This is too warm. You must consider the whole picture, *n'est-ce pas?* You need a multiplicity of colors, an in-
finity of minute juxtapositions. One color affects another,
n'est-ce pas? You cannot put these colors side by side like
that. You need to pass from one to another by fine degrees.
You need some modulation of effect between this brown and
this yellow, this yellow and this white. You need a little
gray here, a little red, *n'est-ce pas?* . . . . This is too much
cut up. You must take into account the relations between
the cool and the warm. You must consider the proper or-
ganization of the whole, the equilibrium. You understand
what I mean? You need to repeat this blue at the bottom.
. . . . There is no reason why these colors should be neigh-

bors. What you need is modulation, *n'est-ce pas?* an infinite number of fine touches.

To one man he said: "You have got too much here, too many little touches that signify nothing. You want to consider the essential things, the general plan—this reflection here, that large band of shadow. What you need is to simplify, *n'est-ce pas?*"

The Japanese had done the model all over in pinks and grays. To him he said: "I don't understand that. What is your reason for transposing in this way?"

The Japanese could find no word of explanation.

"I don't understand that. You may transpose as much as you like if you have a good reason for it. But then, why leave the background in this yellow light? Why transpose one part and not the whole?"

The Jap had no word. But as the master went on to the next canvas, he began again streaking the body of Léonie with long ribbons of pink and gray paint.

The master's greatest commendation was for the man who had no sense of color. There were minor criticisms to be made, but on the whole, it seems, this was not bad, this work of dulness and cunning, this dreary monotony of pinkish brown. It even reminded the master of the work of Derain.

As for me, I was very conscious of the model sitting there like Galatea awaiting her Pygmalion. But I kept such fancies to myself. No one else seemed to be aware of her existence.

"What is your reason for that?" said the master, to the oldish man beyond the stove. "You have put all the white in the cloth and all the yellow in the figure. I don't understand that."

"That," said the oldish man, "is because I have been working with André Maurice, and it is what he told me to do."

The master could only gasp.

"It was Maurice who sent me here, and I understood that the two schools were the same."

"Not at all," said the master, "not the least in the world." He was in a very nasty box. There is no one whom he despises more than André Maurice. "André Maurice is a painter whom I respect, and I've no right to contradict him. But if you ask my opinion, I must say that you can't make a figure all of red and yellow. You can't put all your hot colors together like that without any modulation of tones." He gave a glance or two at Léonie and a wave or two of his clay pipe over the offending surfaces.

And all this while the model sat there like a monument, radiating flesh tints.

FLOWERS AND CANDIED FRUIT

X
FLOWERS AND CANDIED FRUIT

THE Italian government pays its heroes with titles and with compliments. The titles are appropriate to their deeds, and the compliments are the essence of wit and poetry. There was the Duca della Vittoria and the Duca del Mare, and more recently there is the Conte della Villaviera. This last is the distinguished aviator, Casagrande; his title is taken from the lonely farm buried in the Adriatic marshes where Casagrande made descent by night to carry out his daring raids. This name will be handed on to his sons and his sons' sons to remind them of the epic deeds of their ancestor. And equally will they prize the words of the illustrious chief in communicating to Casagrande the favor of the king. "I am truly rejoiced," wrote Mussolini with his own hand to the man of wings, "to have you for collaborator in the great emprise of giving back her wings to Italy." Even more honeyed are the Italian words: *"ridare ali all' Italia."*

This is all in the day's work for the President of the Council. He is always ready with the right words, whether to private individuals, to newspaper reporters, or to the representatives of the Society of Nations. He is the great inventor of slogans. In the present juncture[1] he has need of slogans. He has raised the taxes at the gates of towns till the people begin to cry out. "Nero was a good man," your ragged guide will tell you, as he points out the emperor's loge in the Colosseum; "he laid no taxes on the people, and he gave us bread and shows." And Mussolini posts his appeal to the G.A.R.: "We who have survived, we who have come back from war, claim the right to govern Italy."

Some people begin to weary of a "strong" government. Too many deputies of the Opposition have been forcibly prevented from speaking their views. In too many districts the Opposition party has been prevented from naming candidates. The bolder newspapers begin to talk of

[1] The spring elections, 1924, long before the murder of Matteotti and the troubles that followed.

liberty. And Mussolini has his way of reminding them in epigram of the dangers from which he has rescued a country given to license. "Fascism is liberty," one reads on all the walls of Rome. "Fascism is liberty—but not the liberty to assassinate the fatherland!"

Above all, he is ready with the right words to groups of citizens gathered together for the democratic business of listening to a speech. A political meeting seems not to be, in Italy, the boresome affair we have made it in Saxon countries, with our long-winded periods and our safe and scentless flowers of speech. The discourses of Mussolini are as pointed and graceful, as impassioned and colorful, as the orations of Pericles recorded by Landor.

Is it the Black Shirts of the Abruzzi whom he is addressing? He has no hesitation in telling them as "a simple and documentary truth," that their region is the live and pulsing heart of the fatherland, deterred neither by considerations of rhetorical restraint nor by the fear of provincial jealousies. And if this seems too obviously a flight of rhetoric, he brings the matter down to the most practical basis; in ten months of govern-

ment, he says, the Abruzzi have made the least
trouble and given the most help. He speaks of
the new life throbbing in every province of Italy,
and of the decisiveness with which they have
headed off the Russian peril, to which he refers
in epigrammatic phrase: "I have the visible and
plastic impression of a whole people marching
in serried battalions, now that the Utopias of
Asia have been put down forever."

His speech is as brief as one of Pericles, and
ends with an appeal as fervid and dramatic. "Be
faithful, O Black Shirts, to this our revolution.
Tell me, if it were necessary to begin again, would
you begin? [The Black Shirts shout several
times: "Yes, yes!"] If it were necessary to
march toward other goals, would you march?
[Once more they respond with a great cry:
"Yes, yes!"] Very well, then. Let us part with
this oath: If it is necessary, we will give battle
again, and win new victories." (Tremendous ap-
plause, and cries of *Viva Mussolini!*)

How different a voice from that of the President of the Council in France! M. Poincaré is
likewise, it would seem, an effective speaker; one
who speaks to the point, and with a subtlety, a

plausibility, a wit, that are of great strategic value in the present critical juncture.[1] He is capable of turning a figure of speech with gravity and skill. But he does not seem, like the Italian statesman, to be standing under a rainbow and facing romantic horizons. He has two themes: the wrongs of France, and her position of vantage; he deals in facts as obvious and palpable as ruined cities and the occupation of the Ruhr. It is all summed up in his laconic declaration, addressed to Berlin, "We hold pledges, and we shall hold on to them." (*Nous tenons des gages, nous les garderons.*)

This is not simply the difference between Poincaré and Mussolini. The two men are mouthpieces, and they voice not merely the French and the Italian spirit, but most of all, perhaps, the spirit of the moment in France and in Italy. The rhetoric of Mussolini is the flower of the rhetoric of young Italy, which is the growth of poetry and mystical faith. You will read on a poster at any street corner that the Fascisti are "the Praetorian Guards of ancient Rome, reborn through the eternal youth of this gentle adamantine Italic

[1] In the spring of 1924.

stock." Is a Fascist leader in Bologna under suspicion for his reputed independence of the Roman chief? He wires his denial of the report, and his assurances that "no one obeys more blindly than he, nor loves more mystically, the Chief who commands the rebellion of youth and prepares the greatness of the fatherland." There is something romantically pagan about every gesture of this "rebellious youth." Encamped on the sands of the Adriatic, the Black Shirts rise before dawn to plunge in the sea like ancient demigods, and they hail the rising sun with high acclamations, like an illustrious personage. The rhetoric of *Fascismo* draws its nourishment from the poetry of the *Risorgimento* and the metaphysics of Croce and Gentile. It is not for nothing that the Minister of Public Instruction, the man who is intrusted with the practical business of making over the universities and public schools of Italy, is a professor of metaphysics, but one for whom the abstractions of metaphysics are the bright facts of the imagination.

To realize how far I have come from the American university world, I have only to read of the address given by Gentile at Perugia during

the summer, before the civil and military authorities and the representatives of the church and of
the university. His subject was "Saint Francis
of Assisi," and I wondered what this very modern
philosopher could find to say about the medieval
founder of an order of friars. But that was to
reckon without the subtlety an 1 the accommo-
dating spirit of metaphysics in all times, and
especially without the passion for equations of
contemporary Italian idealism. And Giovanni
Gentile found no difficulty in identifying the
Franciscan doctrine of poverty with the liberty
of the creative spirit in the realms of poetry and
art, not to speak of identifying the Franciscan
love for all created things with the (idealistic)
participation of all things in the life of nature
herself and the universe! So, by the special rhetoric of contemporary idealism, is Saint Francis
made an ally of modern metaphysics and Italian
nationalism.

Nor is it for nothing that the most prominent
figure in the popular imagination, after the Dic-
tator himself, is the eccentric poet, D'Annunzio,
the hero of Fiume. A droll instance of this popu-
larity was offered during a recent visit of the

Papal Nuncio to a small Italian town. The people of the town had been duly coached in their rôle of hosts to the distinguished visitor. They were to accompany his progress with suitable plaudits; and they proved surprisingly amenable to suggestion in the matter. But what was the consternation of the authorities, and what the embarrassment of the papal official himself, to hear him acclaimed in the name of the not too religious poet—not *"Viva il Nunzio!"* but *"Viva D'Annunzio!"* The man in the street had heard of the aviator-poet, but not of the representative of the Vatican! And a moment later, when the populace became aware that it was an ecclesiastic whom they were greeting, one citizen was heard to exclaim in a voice of disappointment, "Who the devil would have thought that D'Annunzio was a priest!"

D'Annunzio has been very prominent for some time in the negotiations between the Italian shipowners and the Marine Federation of Labor, having espoused the cause of the workmen, and using all his influence with the government to have adopted a marine pact more favorable to them. All his utterances in regard to this

pact—this fraternal, this most beautiful, this
holy pact, as it was at various times designated
by Signor Mussolini—are in the most ardent
and figurative terms of romantic poetry. The
long delays incidental to such negotiations have
been a sore trial to his patience. He is a man of
headlong temper, and the apostle of will in the
conduct of life. Weakly hope is the great enemy
of man, who should insist that every instant
yield up at once all that it carries for him. And
he reminds his friends in this connection that
he is one "who has always slain Hope before
the feet of Will." His faith is in action, and in
good faith. Learning that certain officers of the
Navigazione Generale Italiana had accepted his
invitation to meet him, he telegraphed them,
"One man of good will awaits two men of good
will, and the arduous problem is solved."

So far as I know, the arduous problem has not
yet been solved; but the long discussion has given
occasion for many displays of Italian eloquence.
It is an eloquence as colorful as Tintoretto, and
as sweet as Bellini. It speaks with the tongues
of men and of angels. The best symbol of it is
the gesture of D'Annunzio in a moment of opti-

mism over this labor dispute. He sent to the
President of the Council a letter and a box of candied fruit, expressing the hope—the prophecy—
that within a few days would be pronounced the
final word in the matter. Fancy Mr. Kellogg
sending a box of candied fruit to Mr. Coolidge!
And when were fine words ever final?

March, 1924

THE OLIVE BRANCH

XI

THE OLIVE BRANCH

T IS long since the Hôtel du Loup was a place to be recommended for its bourgeois respectability, and an ancient Baedeker could not be expected to have taken note of the stages by which its so well-meaning proprietors had been reduced to their present compromises with a shady clientèle. Discretion, thrift, and piety were still their leading virtues, and they had done well enough on these virtues to be sending off their stalwart son to London to learn some more respectable business. It cannot be said that they did anything to disillusion us except for the momentary surprise they showed on seeing us alight, with all our trunks and children, at their side entrance. Even our letter from Paris was not enough to prepare them for this invasion of wealth and family decency. Their other patrons, so far as we could see, never had any children or baggage, not even a suitcase or a *nécessaire*. But there was nothing

else about their establishment to make one uneasy, apart from the trays on the landings in the
morning, garnished with empty bottles instead
of coffee cups, and the fact that we never seemed
to meet upon the stairs any of our fellow-lodgers.
In point of fact we came to no harm whatever in
the Hôtel du Loup, and our only concern was
over what M. Tarragona might think of our
choice of a lodging.

It was evidently a little hard for him to get
it clear where it was that we had put up. But
that circumstance once mastered, he went
through with the matter with a high unconsciousness of anything out of the way that was
a triumph of good manners and kindly feeling.
We were the beneficiaries of a long-standing
friendship between his family and a sister of
Aspasia's. At some critical hour this sister
had shown the right feeling, had performed some
slight service of love which had deeply impressed
the Tarragonas, and no welcome was too cordial
for any remotest connection of so cherished a
friend. M. Tarragona, as we knew, was a man
extremely busy with the peace of the world, up
to his neck in papers and delicate diplomacies,

but he was not too busy to come himself to
fetch us out to La Closerie. He came in state in
his Ford, a battered little car with a smooth-
running engine, admirable climber of hills. And
this ancient and ingenious flivver at once took
on for us the character of a symbol. It was a
symbol of many things: of a discrimination a-
mong values, the deliberate choice of the simple,
the unpretentious, the genuine; a full consciousness of the distinction between ends and instru-
mentalities; an efficiency devoted to non-com-
mercial, to ideal, ends. This was just the machine that Jean-Jacques might have chosen, if
we could imagine him dividing his time between
a pastoral *closerie* and the bureau of the League
of Nations. Only one could never have trusted
one's self and one's family to any Jean-Jacques
with the assurance with which one did confide
them to this modern visionary. M. Tarragona
expressed in every movement the competence of
the business man together with the urbanity of
the man of the world. He could perfectly manage his machine while paying every polite consideration to his guests. In his restless black eyes
he held a map of Geneva as accurate as that of

Utopia. And he inspired confidence as infallibly as he inspired affection.

The modern suburb of Chênes-Bourgeries has not the full pastoral character demanded by a Rousseau, but it has quite as much of that character as is at all compatible with accessibility to a metropolitan city. And we should never have been able to make our way without guidance to the shady, winding Chemin de la Pommière, let alone identifying the entrance to La Closerie. This quarter, this house, and this piece of land were all as symbolic, as emblematic, as the Ford that brought us there. We at once concluded that this was the way human beings should live in a world where international agreements gave a little security to mortal life, and where a due understanding prevailed of the true ends of existence. This square stone house had no pretensions to grandeur, but it did have dignity and self-respect. It was set well back from the street and more or less protected by the grove of firs and oaks that more than justified the name of the place, and the street itself, the Chemin de la Pommière, had a character of privacy that would make a stranger feel that he was intruding. The

front windows give you a frank view of the kitch-
en, with all its shining copper vessels, and you
have to pass through the hallway to arrive at
the more secluded living-rooms at the rear.
These rooms open upon the veranda and command the garden proper, running back indefi-
nitely in a kind of considered disorder, and for a
distant drop-scene the rugged ridge of the Salève,
giving at the same time a largeness and a sense
of privacy to their outlook.

It was there, in the little *salon*, all homeliness
and dignity, that we were introduced to the
family. And a veritable family party we made.
There were four of us, and there were six of them,
including the pretty Norwegian governess, who
had come to Geneva to perfect her French and
to see a little of the world. We should have been
photographed as we sat there in our straight-
backed chairs, for a picture of international courtesy and good feeling. Our boys had been duly
warned how important it was to give a good
impression of the manners of American children.
But not too great a strain was put upon them,
and they were soon let loose into the groves and
brambles of La Closerie to make an acquaint-

ance as best they might with the foreign boys
and girls. The outcome proved that international misunderstanding is the growth of some
period later than childhood.

What gave most the effect of a family party
was the presence of Dr. Tarragona, the father of
our host, a charming old man, breathing courtli-
ness and cordiality, who had long since given up
his practice of medicine in Paris, and had retired
to a life of liberal and dignified leisure in this
sweet suburb of Geneva. He was the only one of
our party who did not speak English or much
understand it. But he had a Frenchman's ready
indulgence of bad French, and a great eagerness
to hear from us about political affairs in America.
I found myself more embarrassed by the topic
than by the language, for some water of oblivion
had washed my memory clean of all trace of
American political names and issues. It was he
who had to remind me that our president was a
man named Harding, and that Lodge and Coolidge and Bryan were other names of prominence.
I did manage to remember that the governor of
New York was one Smith, that he had made a
good record as governor, and that he was a likely

Democratic candidate for president because he was an acknowledged "wet." But that got me into more trouble. The French doctor could not understand how there should be an issue between the "wets" and the "drys" once the principle of the "drys" had been incorporated into the federal constitution. I ventured upon the dangerous ground of the relations between state and national government. I was led to the statement that New York had no law to reinforce the federal prohibition law, and that the military forces of the state were therefore not available for the enforcement of the federal law. And that proved for Dr. Tarragona an insoluble enigma— how a national law might possibly fail to be at the same time the law of one of the constituent parts of the nation. To him such a situation was tantamount to civil war. And for such a dialectic puzzle my French was quite inadequate.

Another subject on which we had a long discussion was the relation between the centigrade and the Fahrenheit systems of registering temperature. For Dr. Tarragona was a scientist and an excellent mathematician, whereas I am neither, and it took him a long time, even with the aid of pencil and paper, to make me understand what is, I am told, a very simple equation. I was at last made to understand the matter, or pretended that I did. But I have never since succeeded in applying my knowledge. And I had to be reconciled to passing a year without ever knowing whether it was hot or cold.

The Tarragonas are a French family, but many circumstances united to give them an international and highly liberal air. Mme Tarragona is an Englishwoman, and the simple elegance of her table showed a well-informed eclecticism which had taken hints from England and France, as well as from the country of their adoption. I gathered that the Tarragonas do not ordinarily serve wine with their meals, that in fact they are rather impressed, beginning with the doctor, with the dangers of alcoholism. But their notions of hospitality led them to offer us a wine as good as the coffee which we had later in the garden. And then the Tarragonas have not always been French. The father of Dr. Tarragona was a Spaniard, and his own talk is colored with allusions to Africa, where he spent many years of service. The son is a very loyal

Frenchman, but he has had the advantage of long residence at Oxford, and he could look with impartial eye upon international questions. He was saddened by the policies of Poincaré, and still more so by the general attitude of the French toward some of the most beneficent undertakings of the League of Nations. He had an unqualified faith in the destinies of the League, however futile it might seem at the moment in the face of French indifference and Italian insolence. He could even appreciate the motives of America in holding aloof, though he thought it a great mistake and a great pity for us to do so. He believed that we shall live to see the day when the nations of Europe will be united in a confederation like that of Switzerland or our own United States. He based his belief on economic necessity and the growing spirit of brotherhood. His father shared this conviction, and his black eyes gleamed in his dark face with the same soft fire of enthusiasm.

Still, we knew how little their views were shared by the average European, and we had not, like M. Tarragona, the advantage of an active participation in the great work to keep up our faith. So that it was a comfort to see with our own eyes something of the offices where the enormous secretarial work of the Society of Nations is carried on. It tended to give substance to the rather cloudy visions of the Tarragonas. We saw the room in which are filed the treaties registered with the League according to the convention by nations of every continent; we had a glimpse of some such august document; and M. Tarragona lowered his voice to mention the great number of treaties already registered in this short time. It seemed a small thing as against the English fleet, the French army, and even the reputed secret stores of German machine-guns. But we were brought up on the parable of the mustard seed, "which indeed is the least of all seeds; but when it is grown, it is the greatest among herbs, and becometh a tree, so that the birds of the air come and lodge in the branches thereof."

What gave us the greatest assurance in the Palais des Nations was our meeting with the librarian of the League—a portent so friendly and familiar that we felt we were in Albany itself, at the fountainhead of librarians. If there is a type of American woman, she was that, with her breezy neatness and smartness, her cordiality and candor. If there is an American business woman, she was that, with her brisk, shrewd, serviceable ways. And she was the very type of American librarian—not the old-school librarian, the anxious custodian of the national virtue, with a New England severity overlaid by sentimental sweetness—she was the new-style librarian, graduate of Bryn Mawr or Columbia, who knows books and their scientific uses. We knew that she would get the right books, and as many of them as the funds of the Society allowed, and that she would keep them well and make them available for the use of serious students. We felt that, on that side certainly, the League of Nations was in good hands. And we had been brought up on the conviction that "the pen is mightier than the sword."

And that led to the revelation of a paradox. We learned that while our Congress, and our President, and our Secretary of State, and Wall Street, and New England, and the Mississippi Valley all agree in taking a supercilious attitude toward the Society of Nations, while they make

broad their phylacteries and draw away their
skirts from all contact with a soiled and cynical
Europe, there are more Americans employed by
the Society of Nations in one or another expert
capacity than there are Frenchmen or Italians or
citizens of any other nation. Devoted men and
women, I have no doubt, but the situation is
ironical. We are very busy getting the rest of the
world in line, but we are determined not to let
anyone bring us into line. There was also a parable of the mote in the brother's eye and the
beam in our own. But it was not M. Tarragona
who rubbed in that moral for us. He is a man of
peace and understanding, and he was content to
say that it was a pity we should hold aloof.

We were furnished also with tickets of admission to the Assembly of the League, and we
came early to insure getting a good place in the
balcony of the Salle de la Réformation. Already,
however, the best places were taken. There was
indeed at one point just room enough in the front
row for Aspasia and me if we could get past a
stalwart young woman who occupied the end of
the bench. But when we undertook to do that,
she informed us in good American that the places

were being reserved for the wives of committee
members. That was, we knew, quite against the
rules. It now lacked but three minutes to ten
o'clock, and it was expressly set forth in the regu-
lations governing admission that places might
not be reserved after five minutes to ten. But
we were awed by the importance of personages
so highly connected, and we retired to seats
farther back. At quarter past the hour the ladies
arrived and took their seats in the front row.
There was nothing in their appearance to distinguish them as persons who should have seats
held for them, and they did not even seem to
take an interest in the proceedings of the Assembly. They spent the whole time of the session reading the society pages of the Paris *New
York Herald*. Ah, well! we are all interested in
society, and doubtless even Geneva is full of
women fighting for a place in the sun! But again
it seemed ironical that the sun of the League
should fall so bright on nationals of a country
that is too good for the League.

It was not surprising, to be sure, that persons
accustomed to these proceedings should have
given scant attention to what went on in the

Assembly. Legislative assemblies in general are far from exciting. They are the emblematic and decorative exterior of the machine. It is in the committee room behind closed doors that the real work of the world goes on, if indeed it be not in some place still more private and inaccessible to the man in the street. The legislatures themselves do little more than register what is already a *fait accompli*, and enunciate the proper sentiments attaching thereto. This was, in the Assembly of the League, a day of compliments and congratulations. The Viennese statesman expressed, in graceful terms and in elegant French, the gratitude of Austria for the generous treatment secured for her by the League, and announced the general results of the financial measures taken. To judge from what he said, these measures had proved highly successful, and it is only the dispatches of December, 1924, that lead one to wonder how he could have taken so sanguine a view in July, 1923. Upon his conclusion, his remarks were duly rendered over again in English. The rest of the session was taken up with long congratulations pronounced in rather bad French by the Cuban president and then repeated by the English president in extremely good English.

What was exciting about this meeting was the bare spectacle of this assembly of earnest men officially representative of the nations of the world. Except for the members from places like Siam and Liberia, they were not to be identified by personal appearance. And even those Liberians and Siamese had little to distinguish them but their color. All these men were dressed alike in the sober business garb of occidental civilization. There was little of the eccentric in cut of beard or other point of style to mark off one race from another, and a fine-looking man stood an equal chance of being a Roumanian, a Swede, or a Bolivian. It was only the seating-chart that seemed to cry out with myriad color, like a map of the world where each country asserts its individuality in pink or green, in orange or mauve. The seating-chart told of diversity enough to suit the most exacting. The uniformity of garb and style was simply the outward sign of that standardization of thought, of political ideals, which is the great feature of modern life. And however much we may deprecate that standardization from an aesthetic point of view, we know that it is the hope of the world. It has been the salvation of America, and why may it not be the salvation of the world? Again we thought of the grain of mustard seed. But this was no little thing, this most extensive effort ever made by mankind to meet together in the interest of understanding and agreement.

On coming out we encountered old Dr. Tarragona, who is a diligent attendant at the meetings of the great assembly. He was glad to walk a block with us in the Jardin Anglais, to sit a moment on a bench in the sun. And as he left us, his personal friendliness broadened into a larger enthusiasm. "I shall not live to see it," said Dr. Tarragona, a little sadly, and then with a brightening of his smile and a flash of his black eyes, "But you—*vous autres, les jeunes*—you will surely live to see that which was predicted by your English poet, '. . . . the Parliament of man, the Federation of the world.'" Those English words he had studied with care, and they were very sweet upon his French tongue.

THE DIRTY STREET

XII

THE DIRTY STREET

SUNDAY morning I walked down the dirty street. It may have been Rome and it may have been Naples. I am sure it was not Geneva, Lyons, or Columbus, Ohio. I had some errand, but I promptly forgot it. Better streets were black with decent bourgeois coming from mass, but the dirty street was violet and green with the woolen shawls of women who had come out to buy provisions for the Sunday dinner. And it was further enlivened by their families, who had all brought their curiosities or their mischief into the street. The boys were throwing copper coins on the pavement to hear them jingle, or to see whether they would come up heads or tails. The little shops were all open, as they must be perforce where so many of them seemed to be the abiding-place of the shopkeeper, and his social club. And moreover the street was lined with carts and booths dispensing oranges and fresh vegetables.

Within three blocks there were two hurdy-gur-
dies going, and five blind fiddlers in one concert
lined against the wall. And no one in the dirty
street declined to drop a coin in the cup for them.
The place was full of a pleasant confusion. The
pavement was muddy and stained with dish-
water from more than one doorway. And the air
was laden with what Aspasia calls the bad smells
of Italian streets. And yet the people seemed
happy, and I'm sure that I was happy, and almost forgot to bring home my pocketful of
oranges.

Aspasia is sorry for the dirty street, and
thinks something ought to be done about it. She
thinks it ought to be cleaned up. But what if the
street likes to be dirty? Cleanliness and order
are, I suppose, aesthetic instincts in their way;
but they do not seem to be primary instincts
with the Latins of the South as they are with the
Teutons of the North. The Latins seem to lay
greater stress on the sensuous elements of beauty.
Perhaps they like animation better than order,
and smells better than cleanliness. Perhaps they
like their smells. I like them, and I bless the mild
climate and the easy notions of hygiene that fill

the streets of Naples with the fragrance of green
things. Dogs know their masters by their smells;
why may not men know, and love, their homes
by the same happy sensuous means? And who is
to be the judge in such a matter?

Perhaps in Dirty Street they look upon disorder as a time-saving device. The Philadelphia
woman who washes down her front steps every
morning has subtracted that much from the time
available for other purposes. And so with anyone who is forever engaged in setting things to
rights. The philosopher bids us consider the true
ends of existence. For himself the philosopher
chooses the contemplative life. The citizens of
Dirty Street may be regarded in the light of humble Platos, who spend their time by choice in contemplation and peripatetic discussion. They certainly seem to have plenty of leisure for standing
around, and it is a business in which they take
great satisfaction. Aspasia considers that there
are many obvious ways in which these poor people, by the application of thought and energy,
might better their condition; and civilization itself, she considers, since the days of Prometheus,
is one grand process of bettering human condi-

tions. She likes to see people getting somewhere. But I say to her: You people who are forever so anxious to be getting somewhere—is it that you aren't happy where you are?

Or perhaps they have a feeling like that of our friend Vacaresco, with regard to restaurants and cafés. He is a Roumanian who, for love of art, has made his home in France, and whom we came to know while he was making an aesthetic pilgrimage to Rome. I know not by what ignoble manual work he had scraped together the sum of two hundred and fifty dollars—to use our measure of value—which he counted upon to support him in leisure for a term of years while he lived the life of the spirit. We were first introduced to him by common friends—fellows of the brush and chisel—when we had come together in the same picture gallery. And we asked them all to take tea with us of an afternoon at Faraglia's, in the Piazza Venezia. But Vacaresco wouldn't come to tea in the Piazza Venezia. There was nothing surly about him, but he simply didn't turn up with "the boys." And he wouldn't come to dinner at the Pensione Boos. He didn't like the sound of a boarding-

house that was lodged, however humbly, in a
palazzo!

When we went to dine with "the boys" in a
back street near the Pantheon, our Roumanian
was there. He seemed glad enough to see us, and
he was the life of our gay party. Well, we had a
very good dinner; we learned to eat spaghetti;
and we spent a most rational evening in high dis-
course. But Aspasia wanted to know, in strict
privacy, why they couldn't serve just as good a
dinner, and why we couldn't spend as rational an
evening, in some place where they sweep the
floor. Is not the life of the spirit consistent with
the introduction of modern improvements?

Well, my dear Aspasia, I must say that I have
great sympathy with the Vacaresco point of
view, and I wish I could make clear to you the
grounds of reason in it. Modern improvements
represent for you a freeing of the spirit from the
bonds of matter. For you they represent a saving of energy; vacuum cleaners, electric wash-
ing-machines, model kitchenettes: things un-
dreamed of in the philosophy of Dirty Street.
And to us they suggest so pitiful a waste of energy! We think of cities and races wholly given

over to modern improvements, pushing up the scale of living, turning luxuries into necessities, so busy saving time that they have no leisure, so passionate in the pursuit of comfort that they have no pleasure in life. Have you not seen them at Nice or Atlantic City? They have spent their youth and strength, and made their money; and now they have come to spend it in the city of pleasure, on the Board Walk or the Promenade des Anglais, and they look in vain for any real value to be got in exchange for their coin. Vacaresco will not come to Faraglia's for tea because he feels there the commercial spirit of competition, with the silly expensive music that goes into the bill, the expensive clothes of the young men, the cold eyes of *pescecani* estimating the cost of your outfit. He thinks of the American family that spends, getting from Cherbourg to New York, more than the sum that he has saved from years of hard work for a little term of freedom.

Oh, I know what searching things you would have to say on your side if we let you have your say. (I myself must have steam-heated lodgings in Italy, or I should never live to sing the praises of Dirty Street.) Oh yes, you would say, we are all the same in our hearts. We all love luxury, rich and poor alike, Bohemians and *bons bour-geois*, and when we sneer at the *pescecani*, it is half envy on our parts. Well, let it be so. It may be that we know our weakness, and that we instinctively hate a world in which every glance is an entanglement. The serious young artist affects to despise the night life of Paris; he wants to make his money last, and get his work done, and come back to his folks respecting himself in his heart. He may be lying about the night life of Paris, but it is a pious lie. And the way he feels about the poor old dirty Café du Dôme is the way we feel about the clean and bright and orderly places of the earth. We're really afraid we might fall a victim to their seductions, and in the fleshpots of Egypt forget the Land of Canaan. We want to walk softly, to keep on the shady side of the street, to avoid comparisons, and avoid distractions. This is no doubt a dreadful confession of weakness. *Mais que voulez-vous?* We make no pretensions to heroism. We are no Edisons, no Savonarolas. We are poor hermits taking to the desert to escape the temptations of the world. And we have no ambition, like that misguided monk of Anatole France, to grapple with the great worldling, Thaïs, in hopes of converting her to the spiritual life.

But after all, it is perhaps at bottom no affair of reason, but something instinctive and obscure. There is something nostalgic in our sentimental attraction to Dirty Street, and something superstitious. We do not wish to lift our heads too high, for fear of attracting the attention of the gods. That is the way, I fancy, that Dirty Street feels about its own case. There is a comfortable security in being humble. The wheel of Fortune, forever turning, can have no terrors for the modest sybarites of Dirty Street; it may conceivably lift them high, but it cannot cast them down. These old-world gentry are no doubt completer philosophers than we, being of so old a civilization. In their obscurity they have outlived so much greatness; they have survived so many catastrophes. They have but to look on smoking Vesuvius and shrug their shoulders. They have but to look on the Column of Trajan, or the Arch of Constantine.

In the evening I passed through Dirty Street at the hour of the lighting of lamps. Black-faced men were carrying in coal in sacks. At the corner the boys were gathered around the cows with their cups to receive their portion of warm milk direct from the maker. All objects and acts referred to the primary necessities of life, and that, in our day, is an aesthetic asset for any street. Religion was much in evidence, itself perhaps the most primary of necessities after the stilling of hunger. There was one Madonna nobly enshrined with fluted pillars, and lights, and pots of geranium. The shoemaker had adorned his cave with the traditional grotto of the Holy Family, and it glowed with candles and electric globes. My most Protestant friends call it idolatry, but I had no feeling but that of envy for those who are able to worship, if they do worship, at such domestic shrines.

Every house had the Madonna on some table or dresser, as one saw at a glance through the open door. For most of the houses opened directly on the street, and the living-room was continuous with the sidewalk, the women nursing their babies or putting up their hair in serene disregard of who passed by. Sometimes there were cooking operations going on, and always there were beds, plenty of beds, capacious bedsteads of brass—there was that much in the way of modern improvements. There was rather too much furniture in these rooms for what Aspasia calls order. But they made attractive pictures in the light of the few candles at the feet of the Madonnas. In the streets there was little light, and the big star that I call Venus winked benignly over the roof tops.

Aspasia says I am romantic on the subject of Dirty Street. And it may be. But what does it mean to be romantic, and why must it be a term of reproach? When we speak of the Romantic movement in literature, we have in mind a reaction of human nature against too much order. And it may well be that there is a normal human instinct for disorder as well as that other normal instinct for order, and that an excess of either condition is bound to provoke rebellion. A contemporary Italian critic has a very interesting theory about the working of the spirit of Life, as he calls that creative force which Bergson calls the *Élan Vital*. Life, he says, in its perpetual free movement of creation, is continually producing forms to express its meaning and vitality; and, once produced, these forms continually tend to solidify, to harden, and intrench themselves against change and innovation; and so, instead of expressing Life, they simply hinder it, since it is the essence of the spirit of Life to be forever creating new forms to express its ever changing and evolving self. A queer theory, is it not, to flourish alongside of the political doctrine of *Fascismo* and the Big Stick, of a system of government which implies the establishment and maintenance of order by compulsion? But singularly like to Carlyle's idea of the eternal tailor forever reclothed, and Carlyle would have been the first to hail Mussolini as the God-sent hero.

I have no desire now to dwell on the paradoxes of philosophy, but merely to let the philosophers remind us how order itself may become a nuisance and a weariness. It is probably for this reason that people brought up in too orderly a fashion are so liable to go to the dogs; that ministers' sons are the devil's grandsons; that there are so often but three generations from shirt sleeves to shirt sleeves. Have we not in Dirty Street stumbled upon the secret of so many of

Time's revenges? Historians have long been trying to explain the fall of the Roman Empire.
Has it never occurred to them to suggest that
the Roman Empire fell because it was tired of
holding itself upright? Perhaps the Romans
were tired of so much order, and simply called in
the Goths and Longobards to give them a little
much-desired confusion.

PRINTED IN THE U.S.A.